Let Us Rejoice In His Love

"Thou Art My God"

To Joanne

Christmas 1981

Thou Art My God

Biblical Affirmations of God's Relationship
to Us, His People — with Additional Poems,
Comments and Prayers

Selected by
Florence M. Taylor

Designed by Gordon Brown

The C.R.Gibson Company, Norwalk, Connecticut

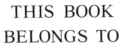

THIS BOOK
BELONGS TO

Table of Contents

To the Reader   7

Thou Art My God   10

Prayers, 13
Now Thank We All Our God, 12
God Is Working His Purpose Out, 14
O, God, Our Help in Ages Past, 15

Thou Art My Comforter   16

What a Friend We Have in Jesus, 17
Prayers, 18

Thou Art My Creator   19

Joyful, Joyful, We Adore Thee, 19
Love Divine, All Loves Excelling, 22
Prayers, 22

Thou Art My Defender   24

How Firm a Foundation, 25
Prayers, 26

Thou Art My Deliverer   27

Great God Who Hast Delivered Us, 28
Prayers, 29

Thou Art My Dwelling Place   30

Who Trusts In God, a Strong Abode, 32
Prayers, 32

Thou Art My Father   33

Lead Us, O Father, in the Paths of Peace, 33
Old Testament Selections, 35
Jesus' Teachings about the Fatherhood of God, 36
The Parable of the Forgiving Father, 37
Selections from the Epistles, 38
This Is My Father's World, 39
The Prayer Jesus Gave His Disciples (Expanded), 40
Thy Kingdom Come, O Lord, 42

Thou Art My Fortress   43

A Mighty Fortress Is Our God, 43

Thou Art My Guide   44

If Thou But Suffer God to Guide Thee, 45
Prayers, 46
Guide Me, O Thou Great Jehovah, 46

Thou Art My Healer   47

At Even When the Sun Was Set, 50
Prayer, 51

Thou Art My Helper   51

Prayers, 53

Thou Art My Hope   54

Prayers, 58

Thou Art My Joy   59

God's Promises, 60
Exhortations, 61
Yet Will I—, 63
My God, I Thank Thee, Who Hast Made, 65
Prayers, 65
Benedictions, 66

Thou Art My Keeper   67

Jesus' Prayer for His Disciples, 68
Prayers, 68

Thou Art My King   69

Come, Thou Almighty King, 69
Immortal, Invisible, God Only Wise, 71
Lead On, O King Eternal, 74
Parables of God's Kingdom, 75
O Worship the King, All Glorious Above, 75
Prayers, 76
Praise, My Soul, the King of Heaven, 77

Thou Art My Life   78

Lord of All Being, Throned Afar, 78
Prayers, 81

Thou Art My Light   82

High O'er the Lonely Hills, 82
God Is Light, 83
Christ, Whose Glory Fills the Skies, 87
Prayer at Sunrise, 87
Prayers, 88

Thou Art My Master   88

O Master, Let Me Walk with Thee, 91
Prayer, 91

Thou Art My Peace   92

Prayers, 95

Thou Art My Potter   96
Have Thine Own Way, Lord, Have Thine Own Way, 96
Prayer, 97

Thou Art My Redeemer   97
Old Testament Selections, 98
In the New Testament, 99
Prayers, 100

Thou Art My Salvation   101
God Is My Strong Salvation, 104
Prayers, 104

Thou Art My Saviour   105
Jesus, Lover of My Soul, 105
Savior, Thy Dying Love, 110

Thou Art My Shepherd   111
Saviour, Like a Shepherd Lead Us, 111
In Heavenly Love Abiding, 113
The Shepherd Psalm, 114
Saviour, Teach Me, Day by Day, 114

Thou Art My Shield   115
In the Hour of Trial, 116
Prayers, 116

Thou Art My Strength   117
My Faith Looks Up to Thee, 118
Prayers, 119

Thou Art My Teacher   120
Spirit of God, Descend Upon My Heart, 121
Prayers, 121

Thou Art My Victory   123
Additional New Testament Selections, 127
I Heard An Old, Old Story, 128
Prayers, 129

**My Prayer for Myself — and for Those
    Who May Read This Book**   129

A Final Word   130

Index   133

To the Reader

This book is the outgrowth of a project in my own, personal Bible study, and was not originally planned for publication; but as I lived with it over a period of several months, I found it so rewarding and enriching, that I felt moved to share it. And now that the labor of researching and writing has been completed, I am aware of an urgency to add a bit of personal testimony.

As I write, I have passed my eighty-fourth birthday. My husband died last year; we had been happily married for almost fifty-nine years. I have three married children, a boy and two girls; nine grandchildren, and three great-grandchildren. For the last almost twenty years I have had the blessed privilege of living with a married daughter and her family — a doctor-husband, and four children — two boys and two girls — ranging in age at this writing from almost sixteen to twenty-five.

Before my retirement, I had been professionally engaged in Christian education for many years — as a director of Christian education in a local church, as a writer of curriculum for several denominations, and for about fifteen years as Associate in Christian Education, with the Protestant Council of the City of New York.

I had always thought of myself as a deeply religious woman! But in my late seventies, I came, much to my own surprise, into a new and richer religious experience.

I came into a new and vivid awareness of God as an everpresent Reality in my everyday life; and into a more personal relationship with my living Lord and Saviour that added a new and lovely depth to my devotional life.

Almost at once prayer became totally different to me. I had "said prayers" all my life, but I discovered that only rarely had I prayed. Occasionally, but very rarely, had I known a genuine, vivid realization of the presence of God. For the most part, as I looked back, my prayers seemed to have been largely formal and dutiful repetitions of words. Too often, I might have quoted to myself the lines from Shakespeare's *Hamlet:*

> My words fly up, my thoughts remain
>   below;
> Words without thoughts, never to heaven
>   go.

As I thought about my prayers, I was also appalled to discover how limited, how lacking in range, and depth, and fervor, my whole experience in prayer had been.

Isaiah's call to be God's spokesman (Isaiah 6) became deeply significant to me, for it revealed with irresistible clarity how varied prayer might be. I discovered that (except for the daily repetition of the Lord's prayer) my own prayers had been limited to petitions for my own wants, occasional intercession for someone I loved, some (but not much) thanksgiving, very little confession and repentance, and *no praise!*

Praise! Why was praise important, I wondered. I discovered in myself a reluctance to praise, almost a resistance to it. There was something almost repulsive to me in the idea of a God demanding praise from His children — in a human parent we would reject the idea as obviously unworthy. And yet, the Bible directives are clear, and strong and frequent: *Praise ye the Lord!*

It was with a genuine sense of relief that I welcomed the God-given insight that it is *not* to gratify God that we are directed to praise Him! (Not that He doesn't enjoy and welcome it! What parent does not treasure expressions of genuine love and appreciation from his children?) But He doesn't need our praises — especially if given grudgingly and from a sense of duty.

Praise is for our benefit. It is *a necessary part of becoming aware of the reality and presence of God.* Thinking about God, meditating on His omnipresence, His omnipotence, His omniscience — all that is fine. But talking *to* Him, expressing *to* Him our love, our dependence upon Him, thanking Him, praising Him — this is better still. This brings to us a vivid sense of His reality, of His immediate presence with us, without which prayer is merely empty words.

So it was out of my own sense of need to develop my

ability to praise, as a way of seeking to become more vividly aware of God's presence, that I began the Bible study out of which this book grew. I sought in the pages of the Bible, and tried to make my own, those prayers and affirmations of God's reality and presence with us which have nourished the faith of God's people for hundreds of years. And in my own experience I proved the truth of the Bible's assurance that "faith comes by hearing, and hearing by the word of God" (Romans 10:17).

The results of this adventure in praise were beyond my expectations. I found myself not only anticipating the times of withdrawal because of the deep joy of my awakening consciousness of God's presence, but I found the joy spilling over into the hours of activity to such a degree that I began to sense "the Holy Companionship" of God in an almost continuous awareness even on the busiest days.

It is my prayer that this book, the writing of which has been a joyous and exciting experience, may prove a blessing to each reader. May God use it to deepen your recognition of His reality, and of His continual activity in our every day lives. And may He draw you ever more closely to Himself.

Florence M. Taylor

Thou Art
My God

Thou art my God: four words frequently repeated in the pages of the Bible; four words of tremendous significance.

THOU — the personal pronoun implies a Person — a Being capable of personal relationships: a "Thou" whom I can know, and who knows me. No impersonal "Creative Force" or "Ground of Our Being" is capable of loving and of being loved. But the Bible asserts that "we love him because he first loved us." (1 John 4:19) He — not It: THOU.

ART — Thou *art.* Our hearts and minds cry out for reality. God is the ultimate Reality — no figment of our imagination, no unreal result of wishful thinking. Reality. "In the beginning, God —" (Genesis 1:1) "Which is, and which was, and which is to come, the Almighty." (Revelation 1:8)

MY — Thou art *my* God. No God, however powerful, however awe-inspiring, can draw me to Him and awaken in me trust and belief and devotion, unless I *know* by my experience of Him that He is aware of me as I am of Him. He must be *my* God.

GOD — Thou art my *God* — the ultimate reality in my life: the Giver of life and death and eternal life: the Source of every good desire; the satisfaction of every need. *Thou art my God!*

Thou Art My God

O give thanks unto the Lord; for he is good: for his mercy
endureth for ever.

Psalm 118:29

Behold, the eye of the Lord is upon them that fear him,
upon them that hope in his mercy.

Psalm 33:18

. . . Be strong and of good courage, and do it: fear not, nor
be dismayed: for the Lord God, even my God, will be
with thee; he will not fail thee, nor forsake thee . . .

1 Chronicles 28:20

For the mountains shall depart, and the hills be removed;
but my kindness shall not depart from thee, neither shall
the covenant of my peace be removed, saith the Lord that
hath mercy on thee.

Isaiah 54:10

Seek ye the Lord while he may be found, call ye upon him
while he is near:
    Let the wicked forsake his way, and the unrighteous
man his thoughts: and let him return unto the Lord, and
he will have mercy upon him; and to our God, for he will
abundantly pardon.

Isaiah 55:6,7

When thou passest through the waters, I will be with
thee; and through the rivers, they shall not overflow thee:
when thou walkest through the fire, thou shalt not be
burned; neither shall the flame kindle upon thee.
    For I am the Lord thy God, the Holy One of Israel,
thy Saviour . . .

Isaiah 43:2,3

. . . ye shall seek me, and find me, when ye shall search
for me with all your heart.

Jeremiah 29:13

11

Now Thank We All Our God

Now thank we all our God,
With heart, and hands, and voices,
Who wondrous things hath done,
In whom his world rejoices;
Who from our mother's arms
Hath blessed us on our way
With countless gifts of love,
And still is ours to-day.

O may this bounteous God
Through all our life be near us!
With ever-joyful hearts
And blessed peace to cheer us;
And keep us in his grace,
And guide us when perplext,
And free us from all ills
In this world and the next.

All praise and thanks to God
The Father now be given,
The Son, and him who reigns
With them in highest heaven,
Eternal, Triune God,
Whom earth and heaven adore;
For thus it was, is now,
And shall be, evermore. Amen.

Martin Rinkart

And I heard a great voice out of heaven saying, Behold,
the tabernacle of God is with men, and he will dwell with
them, and they shall be his people, and God himself shall
be with them, and be their God.

And God shall wipe away all tears from their eyes; and
there shall be no more death, neither sorrow, nor crying,
neither shall there be any more pain: for the former
things are passed away.

Revelation 21:3,4

12

Hast thou not known? hast thou not heard, that the everlasting God, the Lord, the Creator of the ends of the earth, fainteth not, neither is weary? there is no searching of his understanding.

He giveth power to the faint; and to them that have no might he increaseth strength.

. . . they that wait upon the Lord shall renew their strength; they shall mount up with wings as eagles; they shall run, and not be weary; and they shall walk, and not faint.

Isaiah 40:28,29,31

. . . know thou the God of thy father, and serve him with a perfect heart and with a willing mind: for the Lord searcheth all hearts, and understandeth all the imaginations of the thoughts: if thou seek him, he will be found of thee . . .

1 Chronicles 28:9

Prayers

Thou art my God, and I will praise thee: thou art my God, I will exalt thee.

Psalm 118:28

. . . I trusted in thee, O Lord: I said, Thou art my God.

My times are in thy hand . . .

Oh how great is thy goodness, which thou hast laid up for them that fear thee; which thou hast wrought for them that trust in thee before the sons of men!

Thou shalt hide them in the secret of thy presence from the pride of man: thou shalt keep them secretly in a pavilion from the strife of tongues.

Psalm 31:14,15,19,20

O Lord, thou art my God; I will exalt thee, I will praise thy name; for thou hast done wonderful things; thy counsels of old are faithfulness and truth.

For thou hast been a strength to the poor, a strength to the needy in his distress, a refuge from the storm, a shadow from the heat . . .

Isaiah 25:1,4

13

God Is Working His Purpose Out

God is working his purpose out
    As year succeeds to year:
God is working his purpose out,
    And the time is drawing near;
Nearer and nearer draws the time,
    The time that shall surely be,
When the earth shall be filled
        with the glory of God
    As the waters cover the sea.

From utmost east to utmost west,
    Where'er man's foot hath trod,
By the mouth of many messengers
    Goes forth the voice of God;
Give ear to me, ye continents,
    Ye isles, give ear to me,
That the earth may be filled
        with the glory of God
    As the waters cover the sea.

March we forth in the strength of God,
    With the banner of Christ unfurled,
That the light of the glorious gospel
        of truth
    May shine throughout the world;
Fight we the fight with sorrow and sin
    To set their captives free,
That the earth may be filled
        with the glory of God
    As the waters cover the sea.

All we can do is nothing worth
    Unless God blesses the deed;
Vainly we hope for the harvest-tide
    Till God gives life to the seed;
Yet nearer and nearer draws the time,
    The time that shall surely be,
When the earth shall be filled
        With the glory of God
    As the waters cover the sea.

Arthur C. Ainger

14

O God, Our Help in Ages Past

O God, our help in ages past,
    Our hope for years to come,
Our shelter from the stormy blast,
    And our eternal home:

Under the shadow of thy throne
    Thy saints have dwelt secure;
Sufficient is thine arm alone,
    And our defence is sure.

Before the hills in order stood,
    Or earth received her frame,
From everlasting thou art God,
    To endless years the same.

A thousand ages in thy sight
    Are like an evening gone;
Short as the watch that ends the night
    Before the rising sun.

Time, like an ever-rolling stream,
    Bears all its sons away;
They fly, forgotten, as a dream
    Dies at the opening day.

O God, our help in ages past,
    Our hope for years to come,
Be thou our guide while life shall last,
    And our eternal home. Amen.

Isaac Watts

Thou Art
My Comforter

I, even I, am he that comforteth you: who art thou, that
thou shouldest be afraid of a man that shall die, and of the
son of man which shall be made as grass;

And forgettest the Lord thy maker, that hath stretched
forth the heavens, and laid the foundations of the earth . . .

Isaiah 51:12,13

The Spirit of the Lord God is upon me; because the Lord
hath anointed me to preach good tidings unto the meek;
he hath sent me to bind up the brokenhearted, to proclaim
liberty to the captives, and the opening of the prison to
them that are bound;

. . . to comfort all that mourn . . .

. . . to give unto them beauty for ashes, the oil of joy
for mourning, the garment of praise for the spirit of
heaviness; that they might be called trees of righteousness,
the planting of the Lord, that he might be glorified.

Isaiah 61:1-3

For the Lord shall comfort Zion: he will comfort all her
waste places; and he will make her wilderness like Eden,
and her desert like the garden of the Lord; joy and
gladness shall be found therein, thanksgiving, and the
voice of melody.

Isaiah 51:3

Jesus said: If ye love me, keep my commandments.

And I will pray the Father, and he shall give you another
Comforter, that he may abide with you for ever;

Even the Spirit of truth; whom the world cannot
receive, because it seeth him not, neither knoweth him:
but ye know him; for he dwelleth with you, and shall be
in you.

I will not leave you comfortless: I will come to you.

John 14:15-18

Break forth into joy, sing together, ye waste places of
Jerusalem: for the Lord hath comforted his people . . .

What a Friend We Have in Jesus

What a friend we have in Jesus,
    All our sins and griefs to bear!
What a privilege to carry
    Everything to God in prayer!
O what peace we often forfeit,
    O what needless pain we bear,
All because we do not carry
    Everything to God in prayer!

Have we trials and temptations?
    Is there trouble anywhere?
We should never be discouraged:
    Take it to the Lord in prayer!
Can we find a friend so faithful,
    Who will all our sorrows share?
Jesus knows our every weakness —
    Take it to the Lord in prayer!

Are we weak and heavy-laden,
    Cumbered with a load of care?
Precious Saviour, still our refuge —
    Take it to the Lord in prayer!
Do thy friends despise, forsake thee?
    Take it to the Lord in prayer!
In his arms he'll take and shield thee,
    Thou wilt find a solace there.

Joseph Scriven

17

Prayers

Thou hast turned for me my mourning into dancing: thou
hast put off my sackcloth, and girded me with gladness;
    To the end that my glory may sing praise to thee, and
not be silent. O Lord my God, I will give thanks unto thee
for ever.

Psalm 30:11,12

Blessed be God, even the Father of our Lord Jesus Christ,
the Father of mercies, and the God of all comfort;
    Who comforteth us in all our tribulation, that we may
be able to comfort them which are in any trouble, by the
comfort wherewith we ourselves are comforted of God.

2 Corinthians 1:3,4

Holy Father, you are my Comforter. You know every
trial and tribulation of my life — and you have promised
that you will not suffer me to be tempted above what I am
able to handle.
    I thank you for your continual presence with me, for
the sure knowledge of your surrounding love no matter
what dark valleys I must traverse, for the assurance that
"even though I walk through the valley of the shadow of
death" I need fear no evil, for you are with me.
    Enable me, Holy Father, to "give thanks in everything,"
knowing that whatever happens is your will for me. Help
me to make my own Habakkuk's joyous affirmation:
    Although the fig tree shall not blossom, neither shall
    fruit be in the vines; the labour of the olive shall fail,
    and the fields shall yield no meat; the flock shall be cut
    off from the fold, and there shall be no herd in the stalls:
        Yet I will rejoice in the Lord, I will joy in the God
    of my salvation.
        The Lord God is my strength, and he will make my
    feet like hinds' feet, and he will make me to walk upon
    mine high places . . . (Habakkuk 3:17-19)
In Jesus' name. Amen.

Thou Art My Creator

Joyful, Joyful, We Adore Thee

Joyful, joyful, we adore thee,
    God of glory, Lord of love;
Hearts unfold like flowers before thee,
    Praising thee, their sun above.
Melt the clouds of sin and sadness;
    Drive the dark of doubt away;
Giver of immortal gladness,
    Fill us with the light of day.

All thy works with joy surround thee,
    Earth and heaven reflect thy rays,
Stars and angels sing around thee,
    Center of unbroken praise:
Field and forest, vale and mountain,
    Blooming meadow, flashing sea,
Chanting bird and flowing fountain,
    Call us to rejoice in thee.

Thou art giving and forgiving,
    Ever blessing, ever blest,
Well-spring of the joy of living,
    Ocean-depth of happy rest!
Thou our Father, Christ our Brother, —
    All who live in love are thine;
Teach us how to love each other,
    Lift us to the joy divine.

Mortals join the mighty chorus,
    Which the morning stars began;
Father-love is reigning o'er us,
    Brother-love binds man to man.
Ever singing march we onward,
    Victors in the midst of strife;
Joyful music lifts us sunward,
    In the triumph song of life. Amen.

Henry Van Dyke

Thou Art My Creator

And God said, Let us make man in our image, after our likeness: and let them have dominion over the fish of the sea, and over the fowl of the air, and over the cattle, and over all the earth, and over every creeping thing that creepeth upon the earth.

So God created man in his own image, in the image of God created he him; male and female created he them.

Genesis 1:26,27

Praise ye the Lord. Praise ye the Lord from the
heavens: praise him in the heights.

Praise ye him, all his angels: praise ye him,
all his hosts.

Praise ye him, sun and moon: praise him,
all ye stars of light.

Praise him, ye heavens of heavens, and ye waters
that be above the heavens.

Let them praise the name of the Lord: for he
commanded, and they were created.

He hath also stablished them for ever and ever: he
hath made a decree which shall not pass.

Praise the Lord from the earth, ye dragons,
and all deeps:

Fire, and hail; snow, and vapour; stormy wind
fulfilling his word:

Mountains, and all hills; fruitful trees,
and all cedars:

Beasts, and all cattle; creeping things,
and flying fowl:

Kings of the earth, and all people; princes, and all
judges of the earth:

Both young men, and maidens; old men,
and children:

Let them praise the name of the Lord: for his name
alone is excellent; his glory is above the earth and heaven.

. . . Praise ye the Lord.

Psalm 148

As thou knowest not what is the way of the spirit, nor
how the bones do grow in the womb of her that is with
child: even so thou knowest not the works of God who
maketh all.

Ecclesiastes 11:5

For, lo, he that formeth the mountains, and createth the
wind, and declareth unto man what is his thought, that
maketh the morning darkness, and treadeth upon the
high places of the earth, The Lord, The God of hosts,
is his name.

Amos 4:13

Remember now thy Creator in the days of thy youth,
while the evil days come not, nor the years draw nigh,
when thou shalt say, I have no pleasure in them;

Or ever the silver cord be loosed, or the golden bowl
be broken, or the pitcher be broken at the fountain,
or the wheel broken at the cistern.

Then shall the dust return to the earth as it was: and
the spirit shall return unto God who gave it.

Let us hear the conclusion of the whole matter: Fear
God, and keep his commandments: for this is the whole
duty of man.

For God shall bring every work into judgment, with
every secret thing, whether it be good, or whether it
be evil.

Ecclesiastes 12:1,6,7,13,14

For by grace are ye saved through faith; and that not of
yourselves: it is the gift of God:

Not of works, lest any man should boast.

For we are his workmanship, created in Christ Jesus
unto good works, which God hath before ordained that
we should walk in them.

Ephesians 2:8-10

Love Divine, All Loves Excelling

Love divine, all loves excelling,
    Joy of heaven, to earth come down,
Fix in us thy humble dwelling,
    All thy faithful mercies crown.
Jesus, thou art all compassion,
    Pure, unbounded love thou art;
Visit us with thy salvation,
    Enter every trembling heart.

Come, almighty to deliver,
    Let us all thy life receive;
Suddenly return, and never,
    Nevermore thy temples leave.
Thee we would be alway blessing,
    Serve thee as thy hosts above,
Pray, and praise thee without ceasing,
    Glory in thy perfect love.

Finish then thy new creation;
    Pure and spotless let us be:
Let us see thy great salvation
    Perfectly restored in thee:
Changed from glory into glory,
    Till in heaven we take our place,
Till we cast our crowns before thee,
    Lost in wonder, love, and praise. Amen.

                                    Charles Wesley

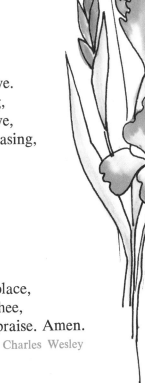

Prayers

Thy hands have made me and fashioned me: give me
understanding, that I may learn thy commandments.

                                    Psalm 119:73

Thou art worthy, O Lord, to receive glory and honour
and power: for thou hast created all things, and for thy
pleasure they are and were created.

                                    Revelation 4:11

O Lord, thou hast searched me, and known me.

Thou knowest my downsitting and mine uprising, thou understandest my thought afar off.

Thou compassest my path and my lying down, and art acquainted with all my ways.

For there is not a word in my tongue, but, lo, O Lord, thou knowest it altogether.

Such knowledge is too wonderful for me; it is high, I cannot attain unto it.

Search me, O God, and know my heart: try me, and know my thoughts:

And see if there be any wicked way in me, and lead me in the way everlasting.

Psalm 139:1-4,6,23,24

O Lord our Lord, how excellent is thy name in all the earth! who hast set thy glory above the heavens.

When I consider thy heavens, the work of thy fingers, the moon and the stars, which thou hast ordained;

What is man, that thou art mindful of him? and the son of man, that thou visitest him?

For thou hast made him a little lower than the angels, and hast crowned him with glory and honour.

Thou madest him to have dominion over the works of thy hands; thou hast put all things under his feet:

All sheep and oxen, yea, and the beasts of the field;

The fowl of the air, and the fish of the sea, and whatsoever passeth through the paths of the seas.

O Lord our Lord, how excellent is thy name in all the earth!

Psalm 8:1,3-9

23

You are my Creator, Lord. Your creative power is moving through me every day I live, in every circumstance of my life.

Grant to me, my Creator, the ability to yield myself totally to your creative power at work within me — that no self-will, no blind stupidity, no rebellious spirit, may hinder your purpose for me.

Finish your creation, Holy Father, and complete me — make me holy as you are holy, loving as you are loving, perfect as you are perfect.

And this I pray in the name of Christ Jesus, your Son and my Lord and Saviour. Amen.

Thou Art
My Defender

My defence is of God, which saveth the upright in heart.

Psalm 7:10

The Lord hear thee in the day of trouble; the name of the God of Jacob defend thee;

Send thee help from the sanctuary, and strengthen thee out of Zion;

Now know I that the Lord saveth his anointed; he will hear him from his holy heaven with the saving strength of his right hand.

Some trust in chariots, and some in horses: but we will remember the name of the Lord our God.

They are brought down and fallen: but we are risen, and stand upright.

Psalm 20:1,2,6-8

Wait on the Lord: be of good courage, and he shall
strengthen thine heart: wait, I say, on the Lord.

Psalm 27:14

. . . the Lord is my defence; and my God is the rock
of my refuge.

Psalm 94:22

Because of his strength will I wait upon thee: for God
is my defence.

Psalm 59:9

How Firm a Foundation, Ye Saints of the Lord

How firm a foundation, ye saints of the Lord,
Is laid for your faith in his excellent word!
What more can he say than to you he hath said,
To you that for refuge to Jesus have fled?

"Fear not, I am with thee; O be not dismayed!
For I am thy God, and will still give thee aid;
I'll strengthen thee, help thee, and cause thee to stand,
Upheld by my righteous, omnipotent hand.

"When through the deep waters I call thee to go,
The rivers of woe shall not thee overflow;
For I will be with thee, thy troubles to bless,
And sanctify to thee thy deepest distress.

"When through fiery trials thy pathway shall lie,
My grace, all-sufficient, shall be thy supply;
The flame shall not hurt thee; I only design
Thy dross to consume, and thy gold to refine.

"The soul that to Jesus hath fled for repose,
I will not, I will not desert to his foes;
That soul, though all hell shall endeavor to shake,
I'll never, no, never, no, never forsake."

K. in J. Rippon's Selection

25

Prayers

. . . let all those that put their trust in thee rejoice: let
them ever shout for joy, because thou defendest them . . .

Psalm 5:11

In thee, O Lord, do I put my trust . . .
    . . . be thou my strong rock, for an house of defence
to save me.
    For thou art my rock and my fortress; therefore for thy
name's sake lead me, and guide me.
    Pull me out of the net that they have laid privily for me:
for thou art my strength.

Psalm 31:1-4

But I will sing of thy power; yea, I will sing aloud of thy
mercy in the morning: for thou hast been my defence and
refuge in the day of my trouble.
    Unto thee, O my strength, will I sing: for God is
my defence . . .

Psalm 59:16,17

Father, how I thank you that you are in all truth my sure
Defender against every seeming evil circumstance of my
life — not that you will keep unpleasant and tragic things
from happening to me, but that your presence with me
will defend me from any evil results, and will give me
strength to live victoriously and triumphantly in the face
of anything life brings.
    Increase, Father, I pray, my sure and unshakeable
reliance upon you, and my ability to give you thanks in all
circumstances, knowing that whatever happens is your
will for me, and that you can bring out of every seeming
evil, accepted as from your hand, a blessing that will
forward your eternal purpose for my life.
    In the name of Jesus Christ, your Son, my Lord
and Saviour. Amen.

Thou Art
My Deliverer

Hear, O my people, and I will speak . . . I am God, even thy God.

. . . call upon me in the day of trouble: I will deliver thee, and thou shalt glorify me.

Psalm 50:7,15

I love the Lord, because he hath heard my voice and my supplications.

Because he hath inclined his ear unto me, therefore will I call upon him as long as I live.

The sorrows of death compassed me, and the pains of hell gat hold upon me: I found trouble and sorrow.

Then called I upon the name of the Lord; O Lord, I beseech thee, deliver my soul.

Gracious is the Lord, and righteous; yea, our God is merciful.

The Lord preserveth the simple: I was brought low, and he helped me.

Psalm 116:1-6

But the salvation of the righteous is of the Lord: he is their strength in the time of trouble.

And the Lord shall help them, and deliver them: he shall deliver them from the wicked, and save them, because they trust in him.

Psalm 37:39,40

Because he hath set his love upon me, therefore will I deliver him: I will set him on high, because he hath known my name.

He shall call upon me, and I will answer him: I will be with him in trouble; I will deliver him, and honour him.

With long life will I satisfy him, and shew him my salvation.

Psalm 91:14-16

27

I will bless the Lord at all times: his praise shall
continually be in my mouth.

    O magnify the Lord with me, and let us exalt
his name together.

    I sought the Lord, and he heard me, and delivered me
from all my fears.

Psalm 34:1,3,4

The Spirit of the Lord is upon me, because he hath
anointed me to preach the gospel to the poor; he hath
sent me to heal the brokenhearted, to preach deliverance
to the captives, and recovering of sight to the blind,
to set at liberty them that are bruised.

Luke 4:18

For I know that in me (that is, in my flesh,) dwelleth no
good thing: for to will is present with me; but how to
perform that which is good I find not.

    For the good that I would I do not: but the evil
which I would not, that I do.

    O wretched man that I am! who shall deliver me
from the body of this death?

    I thank God through Jesus Christ our Lord . . .

Romans 7:18,19,24,25

Great God Who Hast Delivered Us

Great God who hast delivered us
    By thy great love and mighty power,
    In many an evil hour,
Make manifest in this dread time
Thy power supreme, thy love sublime,
    That love that never faileth.

Then to thy name be glory given,
Creator of the earth and heaven,
    Thou bringer of salvation!
To thee, the source of all our joy,
To thee we sing, O Lord most high,
    Glad praise and adoration.

Anonymous

Prayers

For thou hast delivered my soul from death, mine eyes
from tears, and my feet from falling.
   I will offer to thee the sacrifice of thanksgiving,
and will call upon the name of the Lord.

Psalm 116:8,17

. . . I am poor and needy: make haste unto me, O God:
thou art my help and my deliverer; O Lord, make
no tarrying.

Psalm 70:5

Thou art my hiding place; thou shalt preserve me from
trouble; thou shalt compass me about with songs of
deliverance.

Psalm 32:7

Cause me to hear thy lovingkindness in the morning;
for in thee do I trust: cause me to know the way wherein
I should walk; for I lift up my soul unto thee.
   Deliver me, O Lord, from mine enemies: I flee unto
thee to hide me.
   Teach me to do thy will; for thou art my God . . .

Psalm 143:8-10

. . . deliver us from evil . . .

Matthew 6:13

Fill me with the knowledge of your will, Holy Father,
in all wisdom and spiritual understanding;
   that I may walk worthy of you, being fruitful in every
good work, and increasing in my knowledge of you;
   strengthened with all might, according to your
glorious power with all patience and longsuffering
with joyfulness;
   giving thanks unto you, O Father, who have delivered
me from the power of darkness, and translated me into
the kingdom of your dear Son, in whose name I pray.
Amen.

See Colossians 1:9-13

In thee, O Lord, do I put my trust . . . deliver me
in thy righteousness.
    Bow down thine ear to me; deliver me speedily . . .

Psalm 31:1,2

Thou Art
My Dwelling Place

He that dwelleth in the secret place of the most High
shall abide under the shadow of the Almighty.
    Because thou hast made the Lord, which is my refuge,
even the most High, thy habitation;
    There shall no evil befall thee . . .

Psalm 91:1,9,10

One thing have I desired of the Lord, that will I seek after;
that I may dwell in the house of the Lord all the days of my
life, to behold the beauty of the Lord, and to inquire
in his temple.
    For in the time of trouble he shall hide me in his
pavilion: in the secret of his tabernacle shall he hide me . . .

Psalm 27:4,5

Surely goodness and mercy shall follow me all the days of
my life: and I will dwell in the house of the Lord for ever.

Psalm 23:6

They that trust in the Lord shall be as mount Zion, which
cannot be removed, but abideth for ever.
    As the mountains are round about Jerusalem, so the
Lord is round about his people from henceforth
even for ever.

Psalm 125:1,2

For thus saith the high and lofty One that inhabiteth
eternity, whose name is Holy; I dwell in the high and
holy place, with him also that is of a contrite and humble
spirit, to revive the spirit of the humble, and to revive
the heart of the contrite ones.

But the wicked are like the troubled sea, when it cannot
rest, whose waters cast up mire and dirt.

There is no peace, saith my God, to the wicked.

Isaiah 57:15,20,21

Jesus said: Abide in me, and I in you. As the branch
cannot bear fruit of itself, except it abide in the vine;
no more can ye, except ye abide in me.

I am the vine, ye are the branches: He that abideth in
me, and I in him, the same bringeth forth much fruit:
for without me ye can do nothing.

John 15:4,5

. . . hereby we do know that we know him, if we
keep his commandments.

He that saith, I know him, and keepeth not his
commandments, is a liar, and the truth is not in him.

But whoso keepeth his word, in him verily is the love of
God perfected: hereby know we that we are in him.

He that saith he abideth in him ought himself also
so to walk, even as he walked.

1 John 2:3-6

Hereby know we that we dwell in him, and he in us,
because he hath given us of his Spirit.

Whosoever shall confess that Jesus is the Son of God,
God dwelleth in him, and he in God.

And we have known and believed the love that God
hath to us. God is love; and he that dwelleth in love
dwelleth in God, and God in him.

1 John 4:13,15,16

Who Trusts in God, a Strong Abode

Who trusts in God, a strong abode
    In heaven and earth possesses;
Who looks in love to Christ above,
    No fear his heart oppresses.
In thee alone, dear Lord, we own
    Sweet hope and consolation:
Our shield from foes, our balm for woes,
    Our great and sure salvation.

Though Satan's wrath beset our path
    And worldly scorn assail us,
While thou art near we will not fear,
    Thy strength shall never fail us.
Thy rod and staff shall keep us safe,
    And guide our steps forever,
Nor shades of death, nor hell beneath,
    Our souls from thee shall sever.

In all the strife of mortal life
    Our feet shall stand securely;
Temptation's hour shall lose its power,
    For thou shalt guard us surely.
O God, renew with heavenly dew
    Our body, soul and spirit
Until we stand at thy right hand,
    Through Jesus' saving merit.

                      Joachim Magdeburg

Prayers

Lord, who shall abide in thy tabernacle? who shall dwell
in thy holy hill?
   He that walketh uprightly, and worketh righteousness,
and speaketh the truth in his heart.
   . . . He that doeth these things shall never be moved.

                      Psalm 15:1,2,5

Lord, thou hast been our dwelling place in all generations.
   Before the mountains were brought forth, or ever thou
hadst formed the earth and the world, even from
everlasting to everlasting, thou art God.

Psalm 90:1,2

Be thou my strong habitation, whereunto I may
continually resort . . .

Psalm 71:3

Grant, Father, that I may truly make you my dwelling
place in which I live, and move, and have my being:
   where I may find strength to overcome the sin
that so easily besets me;
   where I may find courage to live my life victoriously
no matter what the outward circumstances may be;
   where I may find comfort, when my way lies through
dark valleys, in the blessed assurance of your
holy companionship:
   where I may find amid all the strains and struggles of
daily living, your rest and your peace which passeth
all understanding.
   You are my dwelling place. Thank you, Father.

Thou Art
My Father

Lead Us, O Father, in the Paths of Peace

Lead us, O Father, in the paths of peace;
   Without thy guiding hand we go astray,
And doubts appall, and sorrows still increase;
   Lead us through Christ, the true and living Way.

Lead us, O Father, in the paths of truth;
    Unhelped by thee, in error's maze we grope,
While passion stains, and folly dims our youth,
    And age comes on, uncheered by faith and hope.

Lead us, O Father, in the paths of right;
    Blindly we stumble when we walk alone,
Involved in shadows of a darksome night;
    Only with thee we journey safely on.

Lead us, O Father, to thy heavenly rest,
    However rough and steep the path may be;
Through joy or sorrow, as thou deemest best,
    Until our lives are perfected in thee. Amen.

W. H. Burleigh

Thou Art My Father

The saving and startling concept of the Fatherhood of
God is present in the Old Testament; but it is not until
Jesus' revelation of God's essential nature that the
seed-concept blossomed into its finest and most divinely
lovely expression.

As a surprising confirmation of this, it is interesting to
note that in *Cruden's Concordance* under the word
father there are listed less than ten passages from the Old
Testament referring to God as *father,* as compared with
more than one hundred and twenty-five listed in the New.

Probably by far the most familiar words of Jesus are the
sixty-six words in Matthew 6:9-13 which are known as
"The Lord's Prayer." And perhaps the most loved of
His teachings might be the parable of the prodigal son,
or as it has more fittingly been called, the parable of the
Forgiving Father.

Both of these passages are included in this section.

Old Testament Selections

. . . thou art the helper of the fatherless.

Psalm 10:14

A father of the fatherless . . . is God in his holy habitation.

Psalm 68:5

Like as a father pitieth his children, so the Lord
pitieth them that fear him.

Psalm 103:13

My son, despise not the chastening of the Lord;
neither be weary of his correction:
    For whom the Lord loveth he correcteth; even as a
father the son in whom he delighteth.

Proverbs 3:11,12

Behold, *(saith the Lord),* I will bring them from the north
country, and gather them from the coasts of the earth,
and with them the blind and the lame, the woman with
child and her that travaileth with child together: a great
company shall return thither.
    They shall come with weeping, and with supplications
will I lead them: I will cause them to walk by the rivers
of waters in a straight way, wherein they shall not
stumble: for I am a father to Israel . . .

Jeremiah 31:8,9

Have we not all one father? hath not one God created us?
why do we deal treacherously every man against his
brother, by profaning the covenant of our fathers?

Malachi 2:10

Sing, O heavens; and be joyful, O earth; and break forth
into singing, O mountains: for the Lord hath comforted
his people, and will have mercy upon his afflicted.
    But Zion said, The Lord hath forsaken me, and my Lord
hath forgotten me.
    Can a woman forget her sucking child, that she should
not have compassion on the son of her womb?
yea, they may forget, yet will I not forget thee.

Isaiah 49:13-15

Jesus' Teachings About the Fatherhood of God

In Jesus' Sermon on the Mount (Matthew 5-7) He
refers to God as Father seventeen times. A few of these
references are given below, followed by his parable of
the Forgiving Father, as recorded in Luke.

Ye are the light of the world . . .
   Let your light so shine before men, that they may see
your good works, and glorify your Father which is
in heaven.

Matthew 5:14,16

Ye have heard that it hath been said, Thou shalt love
thy neighbour, and hate thine enemy.
   But I say unto you, Love your enemies, bless them
that curse you, do good to them that hate you, and pray
for them which despitefully use you, and persecute you;
   That ye may be the children of your Father which is in
heaven: for he maketh his sun to rise on the evil and on
the good, and sendeth rain on the just and the unjust.

Matthew 5:43-45

And when thou prayest, thou shalt not be as the
hypocrites are: for they love to pray standing in the
synagogues and in the corners of the streets, that they
may be seen of men. Verily I say unto you, They have
their reward.
   But thou, when thou prayest, enter into thy closet,
and when thou hast shut thy door, pray to thy Father
which is in secret; and thy Father which seeth in secret
shall reward thee openly.
   But when ye pray, use not vain repetitions, as the
heathen do: for they think that they shall be heard for
their much speaking.
   Be not ye therefore like unto them: for your Father
knoweth what things ye have need of, before ye ask him.

Matthew 6:5-8

Therefore I say unto you, Take no thought for your life,
what ye shall eat, or what ye shall drink; nor yet for your

body, what ye shall put on. Is not the life more than meat, and the body than raiment?

Behold the fowls of the air: for they sow not, neither do they reap, nor gather into barns; yet your heavenly Father feedeth them. Are ye not much better than they?

And why take ye thought for raiment? Consider the lilies of the field, how they grow; they toil not, neither do they spin:

And yet I say unto you, That even Solomon in all his glory was not arrayed like one of these.

Wherefore, if God so clothe the grass of the field, which to day is, and to morrow is cast into the oven, shall he not much more clothe you, O ye of little faith?

Therefore take no thought, saying, What shall we eat? or, What shall we drink? or, Wherewithal shall we be clothed?

. . . for your heavenly Father knoweth that ye have need of all these things.

But seek ye first the kingdom of God, and his righteousness; and all these things shall be added unto you.

Matthew 6:25,26,28-33

Ask, and it shall be given you; seek, and ye shall find; knock, and it shall be opened unto you:

For every one that asketh receiveth; and he that seeketh findeth; and to him that knocketh it shall be opened.

Or what man is there of you, whom if his son ask bread, will he give him a stone?

Or if he ask a fish, will he give him a serpent?

If ye then, being evil, know how to give good gifts unto your children, how much more shall your Father which is in heaven give good things to them that ask him?

Matthew 7:7-11

Not every one that saith unto me, Lord, Lord, shall enter into the kingdom of heaven; but he that doeth the will of my Father which is in heaven.

Matthew 7:21

The Parable of the Forgiving Father
    . . . A certain man had two sons:

And the younger of them said to his father, Father, give me the portion of goods that falleth to me. And he divided unto them his living.

And not many days after the younger son gathered all together, and took his journey into a far country, and there wasted his substance with riotous living.

And when he had spent all, there arose a mighty famine in that land; and he began to be in want.

And he went and joined himself to a citizen of that country; and he sent him into his fields to feed swine.

And he would fain have filled his belly with the husks that the swine did eat: and no man gave unto him.

And when he came to himself, he said, How many hired servants of my father's have bread enough and to spare, and I perish with hunger!

I will arise and go to my father, and will say unto him, Father, I have sinned against heaven, and before thee,

And am no more worthy to be called thy son: make me as one of thy hired servants.

And he arose, and came to his father. But when he was yet a great way off, his father saw him, and had compassion, and ran, and fell on his neck, and kissed him.

And the son said unto him, Father, I have sinned against heaven, and in thy sight, and am no more worthy to be called thy son.

But the father said to his servants, Bring forth the best robe, and put it on him; and put a ring on his hand, and shoes on his feet:

And bring hither the fatted calf, and kill it; and let us eat, and be merry:

For this my son was dead, and is alive again; he was lost, and is found. And they began to be merry.

Luke 15:11-24

Selections From the Epistles

For as many as are led by the Spirit of God, they are the sons of God.

For ye have not received the spirit of bondage again to fear; but ye have received the Spirit of adoption, whereby we cry, Abba, Father.

The Spirit itself beareth witness with our spirit, that we are the children of God.

Romans 8:14-16

Behold, what manner of love the Father hath bestowed upon us, that we should be called the sons of God . . .

Beloved, now are we the sons of God, and it doth not yet appear what we shall be: but we know that, when he shall appear, we shall be like him; for we shall see him as he is.

1 John 3:1,2

There is one body, and one Spirit, even as ye are called in one hope of your calling;

One Lord, one faith, one baptism,

One God and Father of all, who is above all, and through all, and in you all.

Ephesians 4:4-6

This Is My Father's World

This is my Father's world,
And to my listening ears,
    All nature sings,
    And round me rings
The music of the spheres.

This is my Father's world:
I rest me in the thought
    Of rocks and trees,
    Of skies and seas,
His hand the wonders wrought.

This is my Father's world,
The birds their carols raise,
    The morning light,
    The lily white,
Declare their Maker's praise.

This is my Father's world:
He shines in all that's fair;
    In the rustling grass
    I hear him pass;
He speaks to me everywhere.

This is my Father's world,
O, let me ne'er forget
    That though the wrong
    Seems oft so strong,
God is the ruler yet.

This is my Father's world:
Why should my heart be sad?
    The Lord is King;
    Let the heavens ring!
God reigns: let the earth be glad!

Maltbie D. Babcock

The Prayers Jesus Taught His Disciples

(Expanded) Matthew 6:9-13

Our Father which art in heaven —
our Father, not mine alone, not the Father only of those
        who claim you by that name, but equally the Father
        of every one of Thy created children — *our* Father:
our *Father,* loving *Father* of all mankind, drawing us to
        Thyself with an everlasting love — our *Father,* who
        makest Thy sun to rise on the evil and on the good,
        and sendest rain on the just and on the unjust; who
        knowest our needs before we ask Thee, and who
        delightest to satisfy them, according to Thy riches
        in Christ Jesus —
our Father which art in *heaven* — in the place of Thine
        abiding, in complete control of all the forces Thou
        hast created, to the farthest reaches of the universe —
        Omniscient, Omnipotent, Omnipresent — and
        intimately present in every circumstance of our lives,
        in every joyous experience, and in those less joyous

but necessary happenings through which we are led
to a deeper realization of Thy reality and Thy
constant Presence:

Hallowed be Thy name —
loving Father Thou art, but also known by many other
    names — Thou art God the Creator, Thou art the
    King eternal, immortal, invisible, the only wise God;
    Thou art Alpha and Omega, the beginning and the
    ending, which is, and which was, and which is to be,
    the Almighty — Hallowed be Thy name.

Thy kingdom come. Thy will be done
   in earth, as it is in heaven —
here in this community, in Thy church, in our homes, in our
    schools, in our institutions, in our places of business —
    Thy will be done — beginning with me;
    and Thy will be done throughout our country, by
    those in leadership positions in local, state and
    national government; and Thy will be done in all the
    countries of the world, until in very truth every knee
    shall bow, every tongue confess the Lordship of
    Thy Son our Saviour, Jesus Christ.

Give us this day our daily bread —
the food we need for the sustenance of our bodies — and
    bread for the starving millions of famine-stricken
    people, daily bread for all of us, please God. Multiply
    the meager loaves of our giving, O Lord, we pray.
And for spiritual nourishment too, we pray for each day's
    supply of faith, and hope, and courage, and love. Help
    us to feed daily upon Thy Word that our spirits may
    be increasingly molded into the likeness of Thy Son,
    Jesus our Lord.

And forgive us our debts, as we forgive our debtors —
our debts, Lord, those we recognize and confess, and those
    hidden sins of blindness and indifference, and lack of
    compassion, sins of which we are not even aware;
    take from us, we pray, every vestige of resentment,

of bitter rememberings and unforgiveness, and enable
us by Thy grace to pray for those who despitefully
use us;

And lead us not into temptation, but deliver us from evil —
we claim Thy promises, O Lord, that Thou wilt not allow
us to be tempted beyond our strength; that Thou wilt
make darkness light before us, and crooked things
straight; And we rejoice that

*Thine is the kingdom, and the power, and the glory, for
ever and ever.* Amen.

Thy Kingdom Come, O Lord

Father eternal, Ruler of creation,
        Spirit of life, which moved ere form was made,
Through the thick darkness covering every nation,
        Light to man's blindness, O be thou our aid:
                Thy kingdom come, O Lord, thy will be done.

Races and peoples, lo, we stand divided,
        And, sharing not our griefs, no joy can share;
By wars and tumults love is mocked, derided,
        His conquering cross no kingdom wills to bear:
                Thy kingdom come, O Lord, thy will be done.

Envious of heart, blind-eyed, with tongues confounded,
        Nation by nation still goes unforgiven;
In wrath and fear, by jealousies surrounded,
        Building proud towers which shall not reach to heaven:
                Thy kingdom come, O Lord, thy will be done.

How shall we love thee, holy hidden Being,
        If we love not the world which thou hast made?
O give us brother-love for better seeing
        Thy Word made flesh, and in a manger laid:
                Thy kingdom come, O Lord, thy will be done. Amen.

Laurence Housman

42

Thou Art
My Fortress

I will love thee, O Lord, my strength.
    The Lord is my rock, and my fortress, and my deliverer;
my God, my strength, in whom I will trust . . .

Psalm 18:1,2

Blessed be the Lord my strength . . .
    My goodness, and my fortress; my high tower, and my
deliverer; my shield, and he in whom I trust . . .

Psalm 144:1,2

In thee, O Lord, do I put my trust . . .
    Be thou my strong habitation, whereunto I may
continually resort . . . for thou art my rock and my fortress.

Psalm 71:1,3

I will say of the Lord, He is my refuge and my fortress:
my God; in him will I trust.

Psalm 91:2

Jeremiah addresses God as: "O Lord, my strength, and
my fortress, and my refuge in the day of affliction . . ."

Jeremiah 16:19

A Mighty Fortress Is Our God

A mighty fortress is our God,
    A bulwark never failing;
Our helper he amid the flood
    Of mortal ills prevailing:
For still our ancient foe
Doth seek to work us woe;
His craft and power are great,
And, armed with cruel hate,
    On earth is not his equal.

Did we in our own strength confide,
    Our striving would be losing;
Were not the right man on our side,
    The man of God's own choosing:
Dost ask who that may be?
Christ Jesus, it is he;
Lord Sabaoth his name,
From age to age the same,
    And he must win the battle.

And though this world, with devils filled,
    Should threaten to undo us,
We will not fear, for God hath willed
    His truth to triumph through us:
The prince of darkness grim,
We tremble not for him;
His rage we can endure,
For lo! his doom is sure,
    One little word shall fell him.

That word above all earthly powers,
    No thanks to them, abideth;
The Spirit and the gifts are ours
    Through him who with us sideth:
Let goods and kindred go,
This mortal life also;
The body they may kill:
God's truth abideth still,
    His kingdom is for ever.

Martin Luther

Thou Art
My Guide

Great is the Lord, and greatly to be praised . . .
    For this God is our God for ever and ever: he will be
our guide even unto death.

Psalm 48:1,14

Is not this the fast that I have chosen? to loose the bands
of wickedness, to undo the heavy burdens, and to let the
oppressed go free, and that ye break every yoke?
    Is it not to deal thy bread to the hungry, and that thou
bring the poor that are cast out to thy house? when thou
seest the naked, that thou cover him; and that thou hide
not thyself from thine own flesh?
    Then shall thy light break forth as the morning, and thine
health shall spring forth speedily: and thy righteousness
shall go before thee; the glory of the Lord shall be thy
rereward.
    Then shalt thou call, and the Lord shall answer; thou
shalt cry, and he shall say, Here I am. If thou take away
from the midst of thee the yoke, the putting forth of the
finger, and speaking vanity;
    And if thou draw out thy soul to the hungry, and satisfy
the afflicted soul; then shall thy light rise in obscurity, and
thy darkness be as the noon day:

And the Lord shall guide thee continually, and satisfy
thy soul in drought, and make fat thy bones: and thou shalt
be like a watered garden, and like a spring of water,
whose waters fail not.

Isaiah 58:6-11

I will instruct thee and teach thee in the way which thou
shalt go: I will guide thee with mine eye.
Be ye not as the horse, or as the mule, which have no
understanding: whose mouth must be held in with bit and
bridle . . .

Psalm 32:8,9

If Thou But Suffer God to Guide Thee

If thou but suffer God to guide thee,
    And hope in him through all thy ways,
He'll give thee strength, whate'er betide thee,
    And bear thee through the evil days;
Who trusts in God's unfailing love
Builds on the rock that naught can move.

Only be still, and wait his leisure
    In cheerful hope, with heart content
To take whate'er thy Father's pleasure
    And all-deserving love hath sent;
Nor doubt our inmost wants are known
To him who chose us for his own.

Sing, pray, and keep his ways unswerving;
    So do thine own part faithfully,
And trust his word, though undeserving;
    Thou yet shalt find it true for thee;
God never yet forsook at need
The soul that trusted him indeed.

Georg Neumark

Prayers

Who is like unto thee, O Lord? . . . who is like thee,
glorious in holiness, fearful in praises, doing wonders?

Thou in thy mercy hast led forth the people which thou
hast redeemed: thou hast guided them in thy strength unto
thy holy habitation.

Exodus 15:11,13

In thee, O Lord, do I put my trust . . .

. . . therefore for thy name's sake lead me, and guide me.

Psalm 31:1,3

. . . I am continually with thee: thou has holden me
by my right hand.

Thou shalt guide me with thy counsel, and afterward
receive me to glory.

Psalm 73:23,24

Thank you, Father, that you are my guide: that I can
safely follow wherever you lead me; that I need fear nothing
that life can do to me, because you are with me always
amid all the confusions and difficulties of my life.

Father, keep my mind and spirit always open to your
guidance; let no lack of attention or concern keep me from
hearing your voice, and no rebellion or self-will prevent
me from yielding myself in complete obedience to your
guidance. In Jesus' name. Amen.

Guide Me, O Thou Great Jehovah

Guide me, O thou great Jehovah,
    Pilgrim through this barren land;
I am weak, but thou art mighty;
    Hold me with thy powerful hand.

Open now the crystal fountains
    Whence the living waters flow;
Let the fiery, cloudy pillar
    Lead me all my journey through.

Feed me with the heavenly manna
    In this barren wilderness;
Be my sword, and shield, and banner,
    Be the Lord my Righteousness.

When I tread the verge of Jordan,
    Bid my anxious fears subside;
Death of death, and hell's destruction,
    Land me safe on Canaan's side. Amen.

William Williams

Thou Art
My Healer

What a mysterious relationship exists between the physical body and the living spirit that inhabits it! We do know from our own experience that how we think has a surprising effect on how we feel.

The Old Testament has a number of instances of miraculous healings. Two that come to mind are: the healing of the widow's son (1 Kings 17:1-24); and the healing of Naaman's leprosy through the concern of his wife's "little maid," — a captive slave from Israel taken by the Syrians (2 Kings 5:1-14).

There are also frequent references to God as a Healer. A few are quoted below:

Bless the Lord, O my soul: and all that is within me, bless his holy name.

Bless the Lord, O my soul, and forget not all his benefits:

Who forgiveth all thine iniquities; who healeth all thy diseases;

Psalm 103:1-3

The recent bicentennial celebration of our country has focussed attention on two significant passages in the Old Testament that are relevant as we consider God as "Healer" in its broadest meaning — one a promise, one a prayer:

If my people, which are called by my name, shall humble themselves, and pray, and seek my face, and turn from their wicked ways; then will I hear from heaven, and will forgive their sin, and will heal their land.

2 Chronicles 7:14

God be merciful unto us, and bless us; and cause his face to shine upon us;

That thy way may be known upon earth, thy saving health among all nations.

Psalm 67:1,2

47

Why art thou cast down, O my soul? and why art thou disquieted within me? hope thou in God: for I shall yet praise him, who is the health of my countenance, and my God.

Psalm 42:11

O Lord my God, I cried unto thee, and thou hast healed me.

Psalm 30:2

Heal me, O Lord, and I shall be healed; save me, and I shall be saved . . .

Jeremiah 17:14

One final Old Testament prophecy about the Messiah bridges the gap between the Testaments:

Surely he hath borne our griefs, and carried our sorrows: yet we did esteem him stricken, smitten of God, and afflicted.

But he was wounded for our transgressions, he was bruised for our iniquities: the chastisement of our peace was upon him; and with his stripes we are healed.

Isaiah 53:4,5

Coming to the New Testament, it seems completely clear that Jesus conceived of His ministry as one to the total person (physical, mental and spiritual). There is His own statement of His "anointing" quoted from Isaiah, and applied to Himself:

The Spirit of the Lord is upon me, because he hath anointed me to preach the gospel to the poor; he hath sent me to heal the brokenhearted, to preach deliverance to the captives, and recovering of sight to the blind, to set at liberty them that are bruised,

To preach the acceptable year of the Lord.

Luke 4:18,19

There are, moreover, all through the Gospel accounts, innumerable instances of healing, sometimes of individuals, often of many people:

. . . great multitudes followed him, and he healed them all.

Matthew 12:15

And Jesus went forth, and saw a great multitude, and was moved with compassion toward them, and he healed their sick.

Matthew 14:14

Early in his gospel, Matthew has this to say:

And Jesus went about all Galilee, teaching in their synagogues, and preaching the gospel of the kingdom, and healing all manner of sickness and all manner of disease among the people.

Matthew 4:23

It is also undeniably clear from the gospel records, that Jesus trained his disciples to carry on this same ministry of healing:

And when he had called unto him his twelve disciples, he gave them power against unclean spirits, to cast them out, and to heal all manner of sickness and all manner of disease.

These twelve Jesus sent forth, and commanded them, saying . . .

. . . as ye go, preach, saying, The kingdom of heaven is at hand.

Heal the sick, cleanse the lepers, raise the dead, cast out devils: freely ye have received, freely give.

Matthew 10:1,5,7,8

And to these seventy also the command was given: "Heal the sick." Nor did these delegated powers cease with Jesus' death. The Acts and the Epistles assume the continuation of these God-given powers in the lives of the Apostles:

And by the hands of the apostles were many signs and wonders wrought among the people . . .

. . . they brought forth the sick into the streets, and laid them on beds and couches, that at the least the shadow of Peter passing by might overshadow some of them.

There came also a multitude out of the cities round about unto Jerusalem, bringing sick folks, and them which were vexed with unclean spirits: and they were healed every one.

Acts 5:12,15,16

After these things the Lord appointed other seventy also, and sent them two and two before his face into every city and place, whither he himself would come.

Luke 10:1

In Acts also we find recorded the Pentecostal experience of baptism in the Holy Spirit, through which these God-given powers were made available (not just to the selected "twelve" or "seventy") but also to other believers in Christ Jesus. (Acts 2:1-18)

All down through the ages, some believers have been claiming for themselves the blessed ability to become channels through which the healing power of God may flow into the lives of His needy people.

The whole area of healing by faith is shrouded in mystery. No one would be bold enough to claim to know answers to all the questions that arise; neither, however, can anyone with an open mind fail to admit that miraculous healings *do* take place today as surely as in the days when Jesus walked the streets of Palestine.

Praise God for His mighty works!

At Even, When the Sun Was Set

At even, when the sun was set,
    The sick, O Lord, around thee lay.
O in what divers pains they met;
    O with what joy they went away!

Once more 'tis eventide, and we,
    Oppressed with various ills draw near.
What if thy form we cannot see?
    We know and feel that thou art here.

O Saviour Christ, our woes dispel;
    For some are sick, and some are sad,
And some have never loved thee well,
    And some have lost the love they had,

And none, O Lord, have perfect rest,
    For none are wholly free from sin;
And they who fain would love thee best
    Are conscious most of wrong within.

O Saviour Christ, thou too art man;
    Thou hast been troubled, tempted, tried;
Thy kind but searching glance can scan
    The very wounds that shame would hide.

Thy touch has still its ancient power;
    No word from thee can fruitless fall;
Hear, in this solemn evening hour,
    And in thy mercy heal us all. Amen.

Henry Twells

Prayer

Thank you, Lord, that you *are* the Healer of your people.
Grant me, holy Father, that your healing power may flow
through my entire being — in my body, in my mind, and in
my spirit. Give me the wisdom and the faith to claim your
promises, and to know the reality of your healing touch
in every area of my life.

Grant, holy Father, that I may also so yield my every
thought and deed to your will, that you may use me as a
channel through which your healing power may flow out
into the lives of people round me. In the blessed name of
Jesus I pray. Amen.

Thou Art
My Helper

Many and lovely are the promises and testimonies in the
Bible of God's always available help to His people in times
of need:

I will lift up mine eyes unto the hills,
from whence cometh my help.

My help cometh from the Lord, which made
heaven and earth.

He will not suffer thy foot to be moved:
he that keepeth thee will not slumber.

Psalm 121:1-3

Be strong and courageous, be not afraid nor dismayed . . .

. . . with us is the Lord our God to help us, and to
fight our battles . . .

2 Chronicles 32:7,8

Behold, God is mine helper . . .

Psalm 54:4

God is our refuge and strength, a very present
help in trouble.

Therefore will not we fear, though the earth be removed,
and though the mountains be carried into the midst of
the sea;

Though the waters thereof roar and be troubled, though
the mountains shake with the swelling thereof.

Psalm 46:1-3

Our soul waiteth for the Lord: he is our help and
our shield.

For our heart shall rejoice in him, because we have
trusted in his holy name.

Psalm 33:20,21

Our soul is escaped as a bird out of the snare of the
fowlers: the snare is broken, and we are escaped.

Our help is in the name of the Lord, who made
heaven and earth.

Psalm 124:7,8

Why art thou cast down, O my soul? and why art thou
disquieted in me? hope thou in God: for I shall yet praise
him for the help of his countenance.

Psalm 42:5

For the Lord God will help me; therefore shall I not be
confounded: therefore have I set my face like a flint . . .

Isaiah 50:7

. . . be content with such things as ye have: for he hath
said, I will never leave thee, nor forsake thee.

So that we may boldly say, The Lord is my helper,
and I will not fear what man shall do unto me.

Hebrews 13:5,6

. . . the salvation of the righteous is of the Lord: he is their
strength in the time of trouble.

And the Lord shall help them, and deliver them: he shall
deliver them from the wicked, and save them, because they
trust in him.

Psalm 37:39,40

Fear thou not; for I am with thee: be not dismayed; for I am thy God: I will strengthen thee; yea, I will help thee; yea, I will uphold thee with the right hand of my righteousness.

For I the Lord thy God will hold thy right hand, saying unto thee, Fear not; I will help thee.

Isaiah 41:10,13

Prayers

Hear, O Lord, and have mercy upon me:
Lord, be thou my helper.

Psalm 30:10

. . . be not thou far from me, O Lord: O my strength, haste thee to help me.

Psalm 22:19

Forsake me not, O Lord: O my God, be not far from me.
Make haste to help me, O Lord my salvation.

Psalm 38:21,22

O God, thou art my God; early will I seek thee: my soul thirsteth for thee, my flesh longeth for thee in a dry and thirsty land, where no water is;
Because thy lovingkindness is better than life, my lips shall praise thee.
. . . my mouth shall praise thee with joyful lips:
When I remember thee upon my bed, and meditate on thee in the night watches.
Because thou hast been my help, therefore in the shadow of thy wings will I rejoice.

Psalm 63:1,3,5-7

O remember not against us former iniquities: let thy tender mercies speedily prevent us: for we are brought very low.
Help us, O God of our salvation, for the glory of thy name: and deliver us, and purge away our sins, for thy name's sake.

Psalm 79:8,9

When thou saidst, Seek ye my face; my heart said unto thee, Thy face, Lord, will I seek.

Hide not thy face far from me . . . thou hast been my help; leave me not, neither forsake me, O God of my salvation.

When my father and my mother forsake me, then the Lord will take me up.

Psalm 27:8-10

Thou Art
My Hope

Webster's *Collegiate Dictionary* gives as the first meaning of *hope*:

Desire with expectation of obtaining what is desired, or belief that it is obtainable.

Hope is more than wishful thinking: it is desire *with expectation*. It is this kind of hope that Paul meant when he ranked it among the three abiding realities: faith, hope and love. (1 Corinthians 13:13)

O love the Lord, all ye his saints: for the Lord preserveth the faithful, and plentifully rewardeth the proud doer.

Be of good courage, and he shall strengthen your heart, all ye that hope in the Lord.

Psalm 31:23,24

Why art thou cast down, O my soul? and why art thou disquieted within me? hope thou in God: for I shall yet praise him, who is the health of my countenance, and my God.

Psalm 42:11

Let Israel hope in the Lord: for with the Lord there is
mercy, and with him is plenteous redemption.
And he shall redeem Israel from all his iniquities.

Psalm 130:7,8

Happy is he that hath the God of Jacob for his help,
whose hope is in the Lord his God.

Psalm 146:5

The hope of the righteous shall be gladness: but the
expectation of the wicked shall perish.

Proverbs 10:28

Blessed is the man that trusteth in the Lord,
and whose hope the Lord is.

Jeremiah 17:7

My people hath been lost sheep: their shepherds have
caused them to go astray, they have turned them away
on the mountains . . .
   . . . because they have sinned against the Lord, . . . even
the Lord, the hope of their fathers.

Jeremiah 50:6,7

It is of the Lord's mercies that we are not consumed,
because his compassions fail not.
   They are new every morning: great is thy faithfulness.
   The Lord is my portion, saith my soul; therefore
will I hope in him.
   The Lord is good unto them that wait for him,
to the soul that seeketh him.
   It is good that a man should both hope and quietly wait
for the salvation of the Lord.

Lamentations 3:22-26

Hope is a recurring theme in the Epistles. Paul begins his
first letter to Timothy with these words:
   Paul, an apostle of Jesus Christ by the commandment of
God our Saviour, and Lord Jesus Christ, which is our hope;
   Unto Timothy, my own son in the faith: Grace, mercy,
and peace, from God our Father and Jesus Christ our Lord.

1 Timothy 1:1,2

. . . the day of the Lord is near in the valley of decision.

The sun and the moon shall be darkened, and the stars shall withdraw their shining.

The Lord also shall roar out of Zion, and utter his voice from Jerusalem; and the heavens and the earth shall shake: but the Lord will be the hope of his people, and the strength of the children of Israel.

Joel 3:14-16

Therefore being justified by faith, we have peace with God through our Lord Jesus Christ:

By whom also we have access by faith into this grace wherein we stand, and rejoice in hope of the glory of God.

And not only so, but we glory in tribulations also: knowing that tribulation worketh patience;

And patience, experience; and experience, hope:

And hope maketh not ashamed; because the love of God is shed abroad in our hearts by the Holy Ghost which is given unto us.

Romans 5:1-5

For we are saved by hope: but hope that is seen is not hope: for what a man seeth, why doth he yet hope for?

But if we hope for that we see not, then do we with patience wait for it.

And we know that all things work together for good to them that love God, to them who are the called according to his purpose.

Romans 8:24,25,28

Wherefore I also, after I heard of your faith in the Lord Jesus, and love unto all the saints,

Cease not to give thanks for you, making mention of you in my prayers;

That the God of our Lord Jesus Christ, the Father of glory, may give unto you the spirit of wisdom and revelation in the knowledge of him:

The eyes of your understanding being enlightened; that ye may know what is the hope of his calling, and what the riches of the glory of his inheritance in the saints,

And what is the exceeding greatness of his power to

us-ward who believe, according to the working of his mighty power,

Which he wrought in Christ, when he raised him from the dead . . .

Ephesians 1:15-20

For the grace of God that bringeth salvation hath appeared to all men,

Teaching us that, denying ungodliness and worldly lusts, we should live soberly, righteously, and godly, in this present world;

Looking for that blessed hope, and the glorious appearing of the great God and our Saviour Jesus Christ;

Who gave himself for us, that he might redeem us from all iniquity, and purify unto himself a peculiar people, zealous of good works.

Titus 2:11-14

Now the God of hope fill you with all joy and peace in believing, that ye may abound in hope, through the power of the Holy Ghost.

Romans 15:13

There is a special word for parents (and grandparents) in Psalm 78:

I will open my mouth in a parable: I will utter dark sayings of old:

Which we have heard and known, and our fathers have told us.

We will not hide them from their children, shewing to the generation to come the praises of the Lord, and his strength, and his wonderful works that he hath done.

For he established a testimony in Jacob, and appointed a law in Israel, which he commanded our fathers, that they should make them known to their children:

That the generation to come might know them, even the children which should be born; who should arise and declare them to their children:

That they might set their hope in God, and not forget the works of God, but keep his commandments.

Psalm 78:2-7

. . . let us, who are of the day, be sober, putting on the
breastplate of faith and love; and for an helmet, the hope
of salvation.

1 Thessalonians 5:8

Now our Lord Jesus Christ himself, and God, even our
Father, which hath loved us, and hath given us everlasting
consolation and good hope through grace,
    Comfort your hearts, and stablish you in every good
word and work.

2 Thessalonians 2:16,17

Prayers

Let thy mercy, O Lord, be upon us, according
as we hope in thee.

Psalm 33:22

. . . in thee, O Lord, do I hope: thou wilt hear,
O Lord my God.

Psalm 38:15

In thee, O Lord, do I put my trust: let me never be put
to confusion.
    Deliver me, O my God, out of the hand of the wicked,
out of the hand of the unrighteous and cruel man.
    For thou art my hope, O Lord God: thou art my trust
from my youth.
    Let my mouth be filled with thy praise and with thy
honour all the day.
    O God, be not far from me: O my God, make haste
for my help.
    But I will hope continually, and will yet praise thee
more and more.
    . . . O God, who is like unto thee!

Psalm 71:1,4,5,8,12,14,19

O Lord, the hope of Israel, all that forsake thee shall be
ashamed . . . because they have forsaken the Lord, the
fountain of living waters.

Heal me, O Lord, and I shall be healed; save me, and
I shall be saved: for thou art my praise.

Be not a terror unto me: thou art my hope in the day
of evil.

Jeremiah 17:13,14,17

Thou Art
My Joy

The Bible is the most joyous book in sacred literature.
The New Testament reveals Christianity as the most joyful
of world religions.

Almost at the beginning of the New Testament the note
of gladness was sounded. The worshipping wise men
rejoiced to find again the star that had led them to
Bethlehem. (Matthew 2:10) Mary rejoiced that God her
Saviour had looked upon her lowly estate (Luke 1:47);
angels announced their "good tidings of great joy" which
was to "all people" (Luke 2:10). Jesus came into the
world, that his joy might be established in men and made
complete (John 15:11). He cured paralytics, who leaped
for gladness. For the "joy that was set before him, he
endured the cross" (Hebrews 12:2). When his disciples
found themselves successful in furthering his Kingdom,
they were filled with joy (Acts 13:52, 15:3). To Paul the
Kingdom *was* joy, as well as righteousness and peace
(Romans 14:17). The fellowship of 1st century Christians
was marked by joy, as stressed in the three letters of John
(I John 1:4, II John 12); who felt no greater happiness
than in hearing that his "children" were walking in the
truth (III John 4). Joy was included in the apostolic
benedictions, as in Jude 24; Romans 15:13.

Madeleine S. Miller
and J. Lane Miller

59

It is amazing how much the Bible says about *joy!* And how its explicit teaching about joy has been largely ignored, or twisted, or misrepresented!

The difficulty in writing this section has not been to find appropriate Biblical passages — the Concordance lists dozens of references under *joy, gladness, rejoicing.* The difficulty has been how to select and organize the wealth of material discovered.

God's Promises

The righteous shall be glad in the Lord, and shall trust in him; and all the upright in heart shall glory.

Psalm 64:10

And the ransomed of the Lord shall return, and come to Zion with songs and everlasting joy upon their heads: they shall obtain joy and gladness, and sorrow and sighing shall flee away.

Isaiah 35:10

For the Lord shall comfort Zion: he will comfort all her waste places; and he will make her wilderness like Eden, and her desert like the garden of the Lord; joy and gladness shall be found therein, thanksgiving, and the voice of melody.

Isaiah 51:3

For, behold, I create new heavens and a new earth: and the former shall not be remembered, nor come into mind.

But be ye glad and rejoice for ever in that which I create: for, behold, I create Jerusalem a rejoicing, and her people a joy.

Isaiah 65:17,18

. . . ye shall go out with joy, and be led forth with peace: the mountains and the hills shall break forth before you into singing, and all the trees of the field shall clap their hands.

Isaiah 55:12

Exhortations

Rejoice in the Lord, O ye righteous: for praise is comely
for the upright.

Psalm 33:1

Let the heavens be glad, and let the earth rejoice: and let
men say among the nations, The Lord reigneth.

1 Chronicles 16:31

The Lord reigneth; let the earth rejoice; let the multitude
of isles be glad thereof.
   The heavens declare his righteousness, and all the
people see his glory.
   Light is sown for the righteous, and gladness for the
upright in heart.
   Rejoice in the Lord, ye righteous; and give thanks at
the remembrance of his holiness.

Psalm 97:1,6,11,12

Sing unto the Lord, O ye saints of his, and give thanks
at the remembrance of his holiness.
   . . . weeping may endure for a night, but joy cometh
in the morning.

Psalm 30:4,5

Glory ye in his holy name: let the heart of them rejoice
that seek the Lord.

1 Chronicles 16:10

Be glad in the Lord, and rejoice, ye righteous: and shout
for joy, all ye that are upright in heart.

Psalm 32:11

Make a joyful noise unto the Lord, all the earth: make
a loud noise, and rejoice, and sing praise.

Psalm 98:4

Make a joyful noise unto the Lord, all ye lands.
   Serve the Lord with gladness: come before his
presence with singing.

Psalm 100:1,2

. . . let the righteous be glad; let them rejoice before God:
yea, let them exceedingly rejoice.

Sing unto God, sing praises to his name: extol him that
rideth upon the heavens . . . and rejoice before him.

Psalm 68:3,4

Let the heavens rejoice, and let the earth be glad; let the
sea roar, and the fulness thereof.

Let the field be joyful, and all that is therein: then
shall all the trees of the wood rejoice

Before the Lord: for he cometh, for he cometh to judge
the earth: he shall judge the world with righteousness,
and the people with his truth.

Psalm 96:11-13

O give thanks unto the Lord; call upon his name: make
known his deeds among the people.

Sing unto him, sing psalms unto him: talk ye of all
his wondrous works.

Glory ye in his holy name: let the heart of them
rejoice that seek the Lord.

Psalm 105:1-3

. . . the joy of the Lord is your strength.

Nehemiah 8:10

Be glad then, ye children of Zion, and rejoice in the Lord
your God: for he hath given you the former rain
moderately, and he will cause to come down for you the
rain, the former rain, and the latter rain . . .

Joel 2:23

Blessed are they which are persecuted for righteousness'
sake: for theirs is the kingdom of heaven.

Blessed are ye, when men shall revile you, and
persecute you, and shall say all manner of evil against
you falsely, for my sake.

Rejoice, and be exceeding glad: for great is your
reward in heaven: for so persecuted they the prophets
which were before you.

Matthew 5:10-12

Jesus said: As the Father hath loved me, so have I loved you: continue ye in my love.

If ye keep my commandments, ye shall abide in my love; even as I have kept my Father's commandments, and abide in his love.

These things have I spoken unto you, that my joy might remain in you, and that your joy might be full.

John 15:9-11

. . . the kingdom of God is not meat and drink; but righteousness, and peace, and joy in the Holy Ghost.

Romans 14:17

Rejoice in the Lord alway: and again I say, Rejoice.

Philippians 4:4

Beloved, think it not strange concerning the fiery trial which is to try you, as though some strange thing happened unto you:

But rejoice, inasmuch as ye are partakers of Christ's sufferings; that, when his glory shall be revealed, ye may be glad also with exceeding joy.

1 Peter 4:12,13

Rejoice evermore.

1 Thessalonians 5:16

Yet Will I —

This is the day which the Lord hath made; we will rejoice and be glad in it.

Psalm 118:24

Thou hast put gladness in my heart . . .

Psalm 4:7

I will sing unto the Lord as long as I live: I will sing praise to my God while I have my being.

My meditation of him shall be sweet: I will be glad in the Lord.

Psalm 104:33,34

Although the fig tree shall not blossom, neither shall fruit be in the vines; the labour of the olive shall fail, and the fields shall yield no meat; the flock shall be cut off from the fold, and there shall be no herd in the stalls:

Yet I will rejoice in the Lord, I will joy in the God of my salvation.

The Lord God is my strength, and he will make my feet like hinds' feet, and he will make me to walk upon mine high places.

Habakkuk 3:17-19

I have set the Lord always before me: because he is at my right hand, I shall not be moved.

Therefore my heart is glad, and my glory rejoiceth . . .

Psalm 16:8,9

The Lord hath done great things for us; whereof we are glad.

Psalm 126:3

. . . my soul shall be joyful in the Lord: it shall rejoice in his salvation.

Psalm 35:9

I will greatly rejoice in the Lord, my soul shall be joyful
in my God; for he hath clothed me with the garments of
salvation, he hath covered me with the robe of
righteousness . . .

    For as the earth bringeth forth her bud, and as the
garden causeth the things that are sown in it to spring
forth; so the Lord God will cause righteousness and praise
to spring forth before all the nations.

Isaiah 61:10,11

My God, I Thank Thee

My God, I thank thee, who hast made
    The earth so bright,
So full of splendor and of joy,
    Beauty and light;
So many glorious things are here,
    Noble and right.

I thank thee, too, that thou hast made
    Joy to abound,
So many gentle thoughts and deeds
    Circling us round,
That in the darkest spot of earth
    Some love is found.

I thank thee more that all our joy
    Is touched with pain;
That shadows fall on brightest hours,
    That thorns remain;
So that earth's bliss may be our guide,
    And not our chain.

I thank thee, Lord, that thou hast kept
    The best in store;
We have enough, yet not too much
    To long for more;
A yearning for a deeper peace
    Not known before. Amen.

Adelaide A. Proctor

Prayers

O satisfy us early with thy mercy; that we may rejoice and
be glad all our days.

    Make us glad according to the days wherein thou hast
afflicted us, and the years wherein we have seen evil.

Psalm 90:14,15

I will praise thee, O Lord, with my whole heart; I will
shew forth all thy marvellous works.

    I will be glad and rejoice in thee: I will sing praise
to thy name, O thou most High.

Psalm 9:1,2

. . . let all those that put their trust in thee rejoice:
let them ever shout for joy, because thou defendest them:
let them also that love thy name be joyful in thee.

Psalm 5:11

Thou hast turned for me my mourning into dancing: thou
hast put off my sackcloth, and girded me with gladness;
　　To the end that my glory may sing praise to thee, and not
be silent. O Lord my God, I will give thanks
unto thee for ever.

Psalm 30:11,12

Thou wilt shew me the path of life: in thy presence is
fulness of joy; at thy right hand there are pleasures
for evermore.

Psalm 16:11

I will be glad and rejoice in thy mercy . . .

Psalm 31:7

Benedictions

Now unto him that is able to keep you from falling,
and to present you faultless before the presence of his
glory with exceeding joy,
　　To the only wise God our Saviour, be glory and majesty,
dominion and power, both now and ever. Amen.

Jude 24,25

Now the God of hope fill you with all joy and peace in
believing, that ye may abound in hope, through the power
of the Holy Ghost.

Romans 15:13

Blessed be the God and Father of our Lord Jesus Christ . . .
　　Whom having not seen, ye love; in whom, though now ye
see him not, yet believing, ye rejoice with joy unspeakable
and full of glory.

1 Peter 1:3,8

Thou Art
My Keeper

. . . I am the Lord God . . .

   And, behold, I am with thee, and will keep thee in all places whither thou goest . . .

Genesis 28:13,15

If thou sayest, Behold, we knew it not; doth not he that pondereth the heart consider it? and he that keepeth thy soul, doth not he know it? and shall not he render to every man according to his works?

Proverbs 24:12

There is none holy as the Lord . . .

   The Lord maketh poor, and maketh rich:
he bringeth low, and lifteth up.

   . . . for the pillars of the earth are the Lord's,
and he hath set the world upon them.

   He will keep the feet of his saints, and the wicked shall be silent in darkness; for by strength shall no man prevail.

1 Samuel 2:2,7-9

. . . the Lord is faithful, who shall stablish you,
and keep you from evil.

2 Thessalonians 3:3

Behold, he that keepeth Israel shall neither slumber nor sleep.

   The Lord is thy keeper: the Lord is thy shade upon thy right hand.

   The sun shall not smite thee by day,
nor the moon by night.

   The Lord shall preserve thee from all evil:
he shall preserve thy soul.

   The Lord shall preserve thy going out and thy coming in from this time forth, and even for evermore.

Psalm 121:4-8

The Lord bless thee, and keep thee:
   The Lord make his face shine upon thee,
and be gracious unto thee:
   The Lord lift up his countenance upon thee,
and give thee peace.

Numbers 6:24-26

Jesus' Prayer For His Disciples

. . . Holy Father, keep through thine own name those whom
thou hast given me, that they may be one, as we are.
   While I was with them in the world, I kept them in thy
name: those that thou gavest me I have kept, and none
of them is lost, but the son of perdition; that the scripture
might be fulfilled.
   And now come I to thee; and these things I speak in the
world, that they might have my joy fulfilled in themselves.
   I have given them thy word; and the world hath hated
them, because they are not of the world, even as I am not
of the world.
   I pray not that thou shouldest take them out of the world,
but that thou shouldest keep them from the evil.
   Neither pray I for these alone, but for them also which
shall believe on me through their word;
   That they all may be one; as thou, Father, art in me,
and I in thee, that they also may be one in us: that the
world may believe that thou hast sent me.
   And the glory which thou gavest me I have given them;
that they may be one, even as we are one:
   I in them, and thou in me, that they may be made
perfect in one; and that the world may know that thou hast
sent me, and hast loved them, as thou hast loved me.

John 17:11-15,20-23

Prayers

O keep my soul, and deliver me . . . for I put my trust
in thee.

Psalm 25:20

Oh how great is thy goodness, which thou hast laid up for
them that fear thee; which thou hast wrought for them
that trust in thee before the sons of men!

Thou shalt hide them in the secret of thy presence from
the pride of man: thou shalt keep them secretly in a
pavilion from the strife of tongues.

Psalm 31:19,20

Thou wilt keep him in perfect peace, whose mind is stayed
on thee: because he trusteth in thee.

Isaiah 26:3

Thou Art
My King

Come, Thou Almighty King

Come, thou almighty King,
Help us thy Name to sing,
　　Help us to praise.
Father whose love unknown
All things created own,
Build in our hearts thy throne,
　　Ancient of Days.

Come, thou Incarnate Word,
By heaven and earth adored;
　　Our prayer attend:
Come, and thy people bless;
Come, give thy word success;
Stablish thy righteousness,
　　Saviour and friend.

Come, Holy Comforter,
Thy sacred witness bear,
　　In this glad hour:
Thou, who almighty art,
Now rule in every heart,
And ne'er from us depart,
　　Spirit of power.

To thee, great One in Three,
The highest praises be,
　　Hence evermore;
Thy sovereign majesty
May we in glory see,
And to eternity
　　Love and adore. Amen.

Anonymous

69

Thou Art My King

In recent years, human kings have lost much of their
power and glory, but in Biblical times it was still true that
kings were symbols of unlimited, invincible power. So it
was natural that worshipping people attributed king-like
powers to God. As human kings have become less and less
impressive, the opposite has been true of God's kingship.

    The poet has caught something of this changeless
majesty of God in these lines:

Immortal, invisible, God only wise,
In light inaccessible hid from our eyes,
Most blessèd, most glorious, the Ancient of Days,
Almighty, victorious, thy great Name we praise.

Unresting, unhasting, and silent as light,
Nor wanting, nor wasting, thou rulest in might;
Thy justice like mountains high soaring above
Thy clouds, which are fountains of goodness and love.

To all life thou givest, to both great and small;
In all life thou livest, the true life of all;
We blossom and flourish, like leaves on the tree,
Then wither and perish; but naught changeth thee.

Great Father of glory, pure Father of light,
Thine angels adore thee, all veiling their sight;
All laud we would render: O help us to see
'Tis only the splendor of light hideth thee.

Walter C. Smith

In the year that king Uzziah died I saw also the Lord
sitting upon a throne, high and lifted up, and his train
filled the temple.

    Then said I, Woe is me! for I am undone; because I am
a man of unclean lips, and I dwell in the midst of a people
of unclean lips: for mine eyes have seen the King, the
Lord of hosts.

Isaiah 6:1,5

The earth is the Lord's, and the fulness thereof;
the world, and they that dwell therein.
　　Lift up your heads, O ye gates; and be ye lift up,
ye everlasting doors; and the King of glory shall come in.
　　Who is this King of glory? The Lord strong and mighty,
the Lord mighty in battle.
　　Lift up your heads, O ye gates; even lift them up,
ye everlasting doors; and the King of glory shall come in.
　　Who is this King of glory? The Lord of hosts,
he is the King of glory.

Psalm 24:1,7-10

(Some people have seen in these "gates" and "doors",
referring of course to the gates of the temple, symbols of
the "barriers" that block the entrance of the Holy Spirit
into our lives: barriers of doubt and unbelief, of sin, of
rebellion. These all have to be lifted up before the King of
glory can take possession of our lives.)

　　O clap your hands, all ye people; shout unto God
with the voice of triumph.
　　For the Lord most high is terrible; he is a great King
over all the earth.
　　Sing praises to God, sing praises: sing praises unto our
King, sing praises.
　　For God is the King of all the earth: sing ye praises
with understanding.
　　. . . God sitteth upon the throne of his holiness.

Psalm 47:1,2,6-8

Thus saith the Lord, your redeemer, the Holy One of
Israel . . .
　　I am the Lord, your Holy One, the creator of Israel,
your King.
　　I, even I, am he that blotteth out thy transgressions
for mine own sake, and will not remember thy sins.

Isaiah 43:14,15,25

Now unto the King eternal, immortal, invisible, the only
wise God, be honour and glory for ever and ever. Amen.

1 Timothy 1:17

Forasmuch as there is none like unto thee, O Lord;
thou art great, and thy name is great in might.

Who would not fear thee, O King of nations? for to thee
doth it appertain: forasmuch as among all the wise men
of the nations, and in all their kingdoms, there is none
like unto thee.

But the Lord is the true God, he is the living God,
and an everlasting king . . .

He hath made the earth by his power, he hath established
the world by his wisdom, and hath stretched out the
heavens by his discretion.

Jeremiah 10:6,7,10,12

Give unto the Lord, O ye mighty, give unto the Lord
glory and strength.

Give unto the Lord the glory due unto his name;
worship the Lord in the beauty of holiness.

. . . yea, the Lord sitteth King for ever.

The Lord will give strength unto his people . . .

Psalm 29:1,2,10,11

O come, let us sing unto the Lord . . .

Let us come before his presence with thanksgiving,
and make a joyful noise unto him with psalms.

For the Lord is a great God, and a great King
above all gods.

In his hand are the deep places of the earth:
the strength of the hills is his also.

The sea is his, and he made it: and his hands
formed the dry land.

O come, let us worship and bow down: let us kneel
before the Lord our maker.

For he is our God . . .

Psalm 95:1-7

All the ends of the world shall remember and turn unto
the Lord: and all the kindreds of the nations shall worship
before thee.

For the kingdom is the Lord's: and he is the governor
among the nations.

Psalm 22:27,28

How great are his signs! and how mighty are his wonders!
his kingdom is an everlasting kingdom, and his dominion
is from generation to generation.

Daniel 4:3

Lead On, O King Eternal

Lead on, O King eternal,
    The day of march has come;
Henceforth in fields of conquest
    Thy tents shall be our home:
Through days of preparation
    Thy grace has made us strong,
And now, O King eternal,
    We lift our battle-song.

Lead on, O King eternal,
    Till sin's fierce war shall cease,
And holiness shall whisper
    The sweet Amen of peace;
For not with swords loud clashing,
    Nor roll of stirring drums,
But deeds of love and mercy,
    The heavenly kingdom comes.

Lead on, O King eternal:
    We follow, not with fears;
For gladness breaks like morning
    Where'er thy face appears.
Thy cross is lifted o'er us;
    We journey in its light:
The crown awaits the conquest;
    Lead on, O God of might. Amen.

Ernest W. Shurtleff

Parables of God's Kingdom

And seek not ye what ye shall eat, or what ye shall drink, neither be ye of doubtful mind.

For all these things do the nations of the world seek after: and your Father knoweth that ye have need of these things.

But rather seek ye the kingdom of God; and all these things shall be added unto you.

Luke 12:29-31

. . . The kingdom of heaven is like to a grain of mustard seed, which a man took, and sowed in his field:

Which indeed is the least of all seeds: but when it is grown, it is the greatest among herbs, and becometh a tree, so that the birds of the air come and lodge in the branches thereof.

. . . The kingdom of heaven is like unto leaven, which a woman took, and hid in three measures of meal, till the whole was leavened.

Matthew 13:31-33

Again, the kingdom of heaven is like unto treasure hid in a field; the which when a man hath found, he hideth, and for joy thereof goeth and selleth all that he hath, and buyeth that field.

Again, the kingdom of heaven is like unto a merchant man, seeking goodly pearls:

Who, when he had found one pearl of great price, went and sold all that he had, and bought it.

Matthew 13:44-46

O Worship the King

O worship the King, all glorious above!
O gratefully sing his power and his love!
Our shield and defender, the Ancient of Days,
Pavilioned in splendor, and girded with praise.

O tell of his might! O sing of his grace!
Whose robe is the light, whose canopy space.
His chariots of wrath the deep thunderclouds form,
And dark is his path on the wings of the storm.

The earth, with its store of wonders untold,
Almighty, thy power hath founded of old,
Hath stablished it fast by a changeless decree,
And round it hath cast, like a mantle, the sea.

Thy bountiful care, what tongue can recite?
It breathes in the air; it shines in the light;
It streams from the hills; it descends to the plain,
And sweetly distills in the dew and the rain.

Frail children of dust, and feeble as frail,
In thee do we trust, nor find thee to fail;
Thy mercies how tender! how firm to the end!
Our Maker, Defender, Redeemer, and Friend! Amen.

Robert Grant

Prayers

Thou art my King, O God . . .

Psalm 44:4

I will extol thee, my God, O king; and I will bless thy name
for ever and ever.
    Every day will I bless thee; and I will praise thy name
for ever and ever.
    I will speak of the glorious honour of thy majesty,
and of thy wondrous works.
    And men shall speak of the might of thy terrible acts:
and I will declare thy greatness.
    All thy works shall praise thee, O Lord; and thy saints
shall bless thee.
    They shall speak of the glory of thy kingdom, and talk
of thy power;
    Thy kingdom is an everlasting kingdom, and thy
dominion endureth throughout all generations.

The eyes of all wait upon thee; and thou givest them
their meat in due season.

Thou openest thine hand, and satisfiest the desire of
every living thing.

Psalm 145:1,2,5,6,10,11,13,15,16

Thy kingdom come . . .

Matthew 6:10

. . . Great and marvellous are thy works, Lord God
Almighty; just and true are thy ways, thou King of saints.

Who shall not fear thee, O Lord, and glorify thy name?
for thou only art holy: for all nations shall come and
worship before thee; for thy judgments are made manifest.

Revelation 15:3,4

How grateful I am, Father, that you are my King —
omnipotent, omnipresent, omniscient, and eternal: and
that I am living right now in your everlasting kingdom,
where you are in complete control of every circumstance;
where even evil and tragedy are used by you to forward
your good and redemptive purposes for your people!

Hasten the time, Father, when every knee shall bow, and
every heart confess that you are truly King of us all. Amen.

Praise, My Soul, the King of Heaven

Praise, my soul, the King of heaven;
    To his feet thy tribute bring;
Ransomed, healed, restored, forgiven,
    Evermore his praises sing:
      Alleluia! Alleluia!
Praise the everlasting King.

Praise him for his grace and favor
    To our fathers in distress;
Praise him still the same as ever,
    Slow to chide, and swift to bless:
      Alleluia! Alleluia!
Glorious in his faithfulness.

Father-like he tends and spares us;
    Well our feeble frame he knows:
In his hand he gently bears us,
    Rescues us from all our foes.
      Alleluia! Alleluia!
Widely yet his mercy flows.

Angels, help us to adore him;
    Ye behold him face to face;
Sun and moon, bow down before him,
    Dwellers all in time and space.
      Alleluia! Alleluia!
Praise with us the God of grace.

H. F. Lyte

Thou Art
My Life

Lord of All Being, Throned Afar

Lord of all being, throned afar,
Thy glory flames from sun and star;
Center and soul of every sphere,
Yet to each loving heart how near!

Sun of our life, thy quickening ray
Sheds on our path the glow of day;
Star of our hope, thy softened light
Cheers the long watches of the night.

Our midnight is thy smile withdrawn;
Our noontide is thy gracious dawn;
Our rainbow arch, thy mercy's sign;
All, save the clouds of sin, are thine.

Lord of all life, below, above,
Whose light is truth, whose warmth is love,
Before thy ever-blazing throne
We ask no luster of our own.

Grant us thy truth to make us free,
And kindling hearts that burn for thee,
Till all thy living altars claim
One holy light, one heavenly flame. Amen.

Oliver Wendell Holmes

Thou Art My Life

And the Lord God formed man out of the dust of the
ground, and breathed into his nostrils the breath of life;
and man became a living soul.

Genesis 2:7

See, I have set before thee this day life and good, and death and evil;

In that I command thee this day to love the Lord thy God, to walk in his ways, and to keep his commandments . . .

. . . therefore choose life, that both thou and thy seed may live:

That thou mayest love the Lord thy God, and that thou mayest obey his voice, and that thou mayest cleave unto him: for he is thy life . . .

Deuteronomy 30:15,16,19,20

The Spirit of God hath made me, and the breath of the Almighty hath given me life.

Job 33:4

In the way of righteousness is life; and in the pathway thereof there is no death.

Proverbs 12:28

In the fear of the Lord is strong confidence . . .

The fear of the Lord is a fountain of life . . .

Proverbs 14:26,27

In the beginning was the Word, and the Word was with God, and the Word was God.

In him was life; and the life was the light of men.

John 1:1,4

He that believeth on the Son hath everlasting life . . .

John 3:36

Jesus said: Verily, verily, I say unto you, He that heareth my word, and believeth on him that sent me, hath everlasting life, and shall not come into condemnation; but is passed from death unto life.

John 5:24

Search the scriptures; for in them ye think ye have eternal life: and they are they which testify of me.

And ye will not come to me, that ye might have life.

John 5:39,40

Jesus said: For the bread of God is he which cometh down from heaven, and giveth life unto the world.

. . . I am the bread of life: he that cometh to me shall never hunger; and he that believeth on me shall never thirst.

And this is the will of him that sent me, that every one which seeth the Son, and believeth on him, may have everlasting life: and I will raise him up at the last day.

John 6:33,35,40

Jesus said . . . I am the resurrection, and the life: he that believeth in me, though he were dead, yet shall he live:

And whosoever liveth and believeth in me shall never die . . .

John 11:25,26

Jesus saith . . . I am the way, the truth, and the life: no man cometh unto the Father, but by me.

John 14:6

And many other signs truly did Jesus in the presence of his disciples, which are not written in this book:

But these are written, that ye might believe that Jesus is the Christ, the Son of God; and that believing ye might have life through his name.

John 20:30,31

Paul said: God that made the world and all things therein, seeing that he is Lord of heaven and earth, dwelleth not in temples made with hands;

Neither is worshipped with men's hands, as though he needed any thing, seeing he giveth to all life, and breath, and all things;

And hath made of one blood all nations of men for to dwell on all the face of the earth, and hath determined the times before appointed, and the bounds of their habitation;

That they should seek the Lord, if haply they might feel after him, and find him, though he be not far from every one of us:

For in him we live, and move, and have our being . . .

Acts 17:24-28

Know ye not, that so many of us as were baptized into
Jesus Christ were baptized into his death?

Therefore we are buried with him by baptism into death:
that like as Christ was raised up from the dead by the
glory of the Father, even so we also should walk in newness
of life.

Romans 6:3,4

I am crucified with Christ: nevertheless I live; yet not I,
but Christ liveth in me: and the life which I now live in
the flesh I live by the faith of the Son of God, who loved
me, and gave himself for me.

Galatians 2:20

If ye then be risen with Christ, seek those things which
are above, where Christ sitteth on the right hand of God.

Set your affection on things above, not on things
on the earth.

For ye are dead, and your life is hid with Christ in God.

Colossians 3:1-3

Prayers

Thy mercy, O Lord, is in the heavens; and thy faithfulness
reacheth unto the clouds.

How excellent is thy lovingkindness, O God! therefore
the children of men put their trust under the shadow of
thy wings.

For with thee is the fountain of life . . .

Psalm 36:5,7,9

I will praise thee; for I am fearfully and wonderfully made:
marvellous are thy works; and that my soul knoweth
right well.

My substance was not hid from thee, when I was made
in secret, and curiously wrought in the lowest parts
of the earth.

Thine eyes did see my substance, yet being unperfect;
and in thy book all my members were written, which in
continuance were fashioned, when as yet there was none
of them.

How precious also are thy thoughts unto me, O God!
how great is the sum of them!

You *are* my life, my Father. It is by your power that I was
born, and that I continue to breathe and live — for it is
in you that I live and move and have my being. Thank you,
Father, for life.

It is not only for the life of my body that I am grateful,
but also for my mind and for my spirit.

I thank you for my mind and the amazing abilities
you have given me to think and understand, and to
communicate with others; to question and search for truth,
and to recognize it with deep assurance when I discover it.

Most of all I am grateful for the spirit that you have
implanted in my body — the spirit that recognizes that
you are my Father, and that I am your child.

Help me know in vivid awareness that my body is truly
the temple of your indwelling Holy Spirit, through whom
I am enabled to grow from glory into glory, into the
likeness of your Son, my living Lord. Amen.

Thou Art
My Light

High O'er the Lonely Hills

High o'er the lonely hills
    Black turns to gray,
Birdsong the valley fills,
    Mists fold away;
Gray wakes to green again,
Beauty is seen again,
Gold and serene again
    Dawneth the day.

So, o'er the hills of life,
    Stormy, forlorn,
Out of the cloud and strife
    Sunrise is born;
Swift grows the light for us;
Ended is night for us;
Soundless and bright for us
    Breaketh God's morn.

82

Hear we no beat of drums,
  Fanfare nor cry,
When Christ the herald comes
  Quietly nigh;
Splendor he makes on earth;
Color awakes on earth;
Suddenly breaks on earth
  Light from the sky.

Bid then farewell to sleep:
  Rise up and run!
What though the hill be steep?
  Strength's in the sun.
Now shall you find at last
Night's left behind at last,
And for mankind at last
  Day has begun!

Jan Struther

God Is Light

Our waiting upon God can have no higher object than
simply having his light shine on us, and in us, and through
us, all the day. God is light. God is a sun. Paul says:
"God has shined in our hearts to give the light." What
light? "The light of the glory of God in the face of Jesus
Christ." Just as the sun shines its beautiful, life-giving
light on and into our earth, so God shines into our hearts
the light of His glory, of His love, in Christ Jesus His Son.
Our heart is meant to have that light filling and gladdening
it all the day . . . God's love shines on us without ceasing . . .

   Faith, simple faith in God's Word and love, is to be the
opening of the heart to receive and enjoy the unspeakable
glory of His grace. And just as the trees, day by day, and
month by month, stand and grow into beauty and
fruitfulness just welcoming whatever sunshine the sun
may give, so it is the very highest exercise of our Christian
life just to abide in the light of God, and let it and let Him
fill us with the light and the brightness it brings in. Say . . .
God is light: I shall take time and just be still and rest
in the light of God.

Andrew Murray

Thou Art My Light

For thou wilt light my candle: the Lord my God will
enlighten my darkness.

Psalm 18:28

The Lord is my light and my salvation; whom shall I fear?
the Lord is the strength of my life; of whom shall I
be afraid?

Psalm 27:1

. . . when I fall, I shall arise; when I sit in darkness,
the Lord shall be a light unto me.
    . . . he will bring me forth to the light, and I shall
behold his righteousness.

Micah 7:8,9

God be merciful unto us, and bless us; and cause his face
to shine upon us; Selah.

Psalm 67:1

The mighty God, even the Lord, hath spoken, and called
the earth from the rising of the sun unto the going down
thereof.
    Out of Zion, the perfection of beauty, God hath shined.

Psalm 50:1,2

The people that walked in darkness have seen a great light:
they that dwell in the land of the shadow of death, upon
them hath the light shined.

Isaiah 9:2

Arise, shine; for thy light is come, and the glory of the Lord
is risen upon thee.
    The sun shall be no more thy light by day; neither for
brightness shall the moon give light unto thee: but the Lord
shall be unto thee an everlasting light, and thy God
thy glory.

Isaiah 60:1,19

. . . come ye, and let us walk in the light of the Lord.

Isaiah 2:5

In the beginning was the Word, and the Word was with
God, and the Word was God.
    The same was in the beginning with God.
    All things were made by him; and without him was not
any thing made that was made.

In him was life; and the life was the light of men.

And the light shineth in darkness; and the darkness comprehended it not.

And the Word was made flesh, and dwelt among us, (and we beheld his glory, the glory as of the only begotten of the Father,) full of grace and truth.

John 1:1-5,14

And this is the condemnation, that light is come into the world, and men loved darkness rather than light, because their deeds were evil.

For every one that doeth evil hateth the light, neither cometh to the light, lest his deeds should be reproved.

But he that doeth truth cometh to the light, that his deeds may be made manifest, that they are wrought in God.

John 3:19-21

Then spake Jesus again unto them, saying, I am the light of the world: he that followeth me shall not walk in darkness, but shall have the light of life.

John 8:12

Jesus said . . . As long as I am in the world, I am the light of the world.

John 9:5

Jesus cried and said, He that believeth on me, believeth not on me, but on him that sent me.

And he that seeth me seeth him that sent me.

I am come a light into the world, that whosoever believeth on me should not abide in darkness.

John 12:44-46

For ye were sometimes darkness, but now are ye light in the Lord: walk as children of light.

Ephesians 5:8

This then is the message which we have heard of him, and declare unto you, that God is light, and in him is no darkness at all.

If we say that we have fellowship with him, and walk in darkness, we lie, and do not the truth:

But if we walk in the light, as he is in the light, we have fellowship one with another, and the blood of Jesus Christ his Son cleanseth us from all sin.

1 John 1:5-7

. . . the darkness is past, and the true light now shineth.

He that saith he is in the light, and hateth his brother, is in darkness even until now.

He that loveth his brother abideth in the light, and there is none occasion of stumbling in him.

But he that hateth his brother is in darkness, and walketh in darkness, and knoweth not whither he goeth, because that darkness hath blinded his eyes.

1 John 2:8-11

But ye are a chosen generation, a royal priesthood, an holy nation, a peculiar people; that ye should shew forth the praises of him who hath called you out of darkness into his marvellous light:

Which in time past were not a people, but are now the people of God: which had not obtained mercy, but now have obtained mercy.

1 Peter 2:9,10

For we preach not ourselves, but Christ Jesus the Lord . . .

For God, who commanded the light to shine out of darkness, hath shined in our hearts, to give the light of the knowledge of the glory of God in the face of Jesus Christ.

2 Corinthians 4:5,6

And I saw a new heaven and a new earth: for the first heaven and the first earth were passed away; and there was no more sea.

And the city had no need of the sun, neither of the moon, to shine in it: for the glory of God did lighten it, and the Lamb is the light thereof.

Revelation 21:1,23

Prayer at Sunrise

O mighty, powerful, dark-dispelling sun,
Now thou art risen, and thy day begun.
How shrink the shrouding mists before thy
            face,
As up thou spring'st to thy diurnal race!
How darkness chases darkness to the west,
As shades of light on light rise radiant
            from thy crest!
For thee, great source of strength, emblem
            of might,
In hours of darkest gloom there is no night.
Thou shinest on though clouds hide thee
            from sight
And through each break thou sendest down
            thy light.

O greater Maker of this Thy great sun,
Give me the strength this one day's race
            to run;
Fill me with light, fill me with sun-like
            strength;
Fill me with joy to rob the day its length.
Light from within, light that will outward
            shine,
Strength to make strong some weaker heart
            than mine,
Joy to make glad each soul that feels its
            touch;
Great Father of the sun, I ask this much.

James Weldon Johnson

Christ Whose Glory Fills the Skies

Christ, whose glory fills the skies,
        Christ, the true, the only Light,
Sun of Righteousness, arise!
        Triumph o'er the shades of night:
Day-spring from on high, be near;
Day-star, in my heart appear.

Dark and cheerless is the morn
        Unaccompanied by thee;
Joyless is the day's return,
        Till thy mercy's beams I see;
Till they inward light impart,
Glad my eyes, and warm my heart.

Visit then this soul of mine!
        Pierce the gloom of sin and grief!
Fill me, radiancy divine;
        Scatter all my unbelief;
More and more thyself display,
Shining to the perfect day. Amen.

Charles Wesley

Prayers

. . . Lord, lift thou up the light of thy countenance upon us.

Psalm 4:6

Turn us again, O God, and cause thy face to shine;
and we shall be saved.

Psalm 80:3

O send out thy light and thy truth: let them lead me;
let them bring me unto thy holy hill . . .

Psalm 43:3

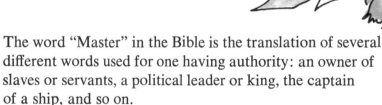

Thou Art
My Master

The word "Master" in the Bible is the translation of several
different words used for one having authority: an owner of
slaves or servants, a political leader or king, the captain
of a ship, and so on.

"Rabboni," frequently translated "Master," seems to
have been the name by which Jesus was usually called or
referred to by his disciples. In some versions, it is translated
"teacher."

The idea of God as "Master" occurs in the Old
Testament, but rarely, as for instance, in Psalm 123:2:

Behold, as the eyes of servants look unto the hand of their
masters, and as the eyes of a maiden unto the hand of her
mistress; so our eyes wait upon the Lord our God, until
that he have mercy upon us.

And in Malachi we find one other instance:

88

A son honoureth his father, and a servant his master:
if then I be a father, where is mine honour? and if I be
a master, where is my fear? saith the Lord of hosts unto
you, O priests, that despise my name . . .

Malachi 1:6

In the New Testament, however, the word "master" not
only appears frequently as applied to Jesus, but there are
several specific teachings which are important for us as
His followers to take heart, if we are to achieve the attitude
of genuine humility, and render Him acceptable service.

When Jesus is sending out the twelve disciples, he
warns them of trials to come:

Behold, I send you forth as sheep in the midst of
wolves . . .

And ye shall be hated of all men for my name's sake:
but he that endureth to the end shall be saved.

The disciple is not above his master, nor the servant
above his lord.

. . . If they have called the master of the house
Beelzebub, how much more shall they call them of his
household?

What I tell you in darkness, that speak ye in light: and
what ye hear in the ear, that preach ye upon the housetops.

And fear not them which kill the body, but are not able
to kill the soul: but rather fear him which is able to destroy
both soul and body in hell.

Are not two sparrows sold for a farthing? and one of
them shall not fall on the ground without your Father.

Fear ye not therefore, ye are of more value than many
sparrows.

Matthew 10:16,22,24,25,27-29,31

Another time Jesus said to the multitude, and to his
disciples:

. . . The scribes and the Pharisees sit in Moses' seat:

All therefore whatsoever they bid you observe, that
observe and do; but do not ye after their works: for they
say, and do not.

For they bind heavy burdens and grievous to be borne,

89

and lay them on men's shoulders; but they themselves will
not move them with one of their fingers.

But all of their works they do for to be seen of men . . .

And love the uppermost rooms at feasts, and the chief
seats in the synagogues,

And greetings in the markets, and to be called of men,
Rabbi, Rabbi.

But be not ye called Rabbi: for one is your Master,
even Christ; and all ye are brethren.

Neither be ye called masters: for one is your Master,
even Christ.

But he that is greatest among you shall be your servant.

And whosoever shall exalt himself shall be abased;
and he that shall humble himself shall be exalted.

Matthew 23:1-8,10-12

One further teaching of Jesus, combined with a symbolic
act, has eternal significance for His followers in every age.
After the Last Supper with His disciples,

Jesus knowing that the Father had given all things into his
hands, and that he was come from God, and went to God;

He riseth from supper, and laid aside his garments;
and took a towel, and girded himself.

After that he poureth water into a bason, and began
to wash the disciples' feet, and to wipe them with the towel
wherewith he was girded.

So after he had washed their feet, and had taken his
garments, and was set down again, he said unto them,
Know ye what I have done to you?

Ye call me Master and Lord: and ye say well;
for so I am.

If I then, your Lord and Master, have washed your feet;
ye also ought to wash one another's feet.

For I have given you an example, that ye should do
as I have done to you.

Verily, verily, I say unto you, The servant is not greater
than his lord; neither he that is sent greater than he that
sent him.

If ye know these things, happy are ye if ye do them.

John 13:3-5,12-17

O Master, Let Me Walk With Thee

O Master, let me walk with thee
In lowly paths of service free;
Tell me thy secret; help me bear
The strain of toil, the fret of care.

Help me the slow of heart to move
By some clear, winning word of love;
Teach me the wayward feet to stay,
And guide them in the homeward way.

Teach me thy patience; still with thee
In closer, dearer company,
In work that keeps faith sweet and strong,
In trust that triumphs over wrong;

In hope that sends a shining ray
Far down the future's broadening way,
In peace that only thou canst give,
With thee, O Master, let me live. Amen.

Washington Gladden

Prayer

Help me, Lord Jesus, to accept with my whole heart the truth that you are my Master. Help me realize that as my Master you have given me inescapable directives in your holy Word for my life. Enable me to read your words in the Gospels as though you were speaking them directly to me, now, in the very circumstances of my present-day life.

Help me to realize that these are not just suggestions, but that they are binding directives, inescapable; and that ignoring or rebelling against them inevitably brings dire consequences.

Help me realize too, that accepting you as my Master, yielding willing and eager obedience to every directive in your Word, and from your living Spirit within me, *also* brings consequences — joyful fulfillment of my deepest desires, growth in grace, and in the blessed privilege of being a profitable servant, and newness and fulness of life. Amen.

Thou Art
My Peace

Many of the Bible references to "peace" have to do with international relationships. There is, however, another kind of peace — the peace of an individual heart. And it is that kind with which this section deals.

The Lord bless thee, and keep thee:
   The Lord make his face shine upon thee, and be gracious unto thee:
   The Lord lift up his countenance upon thee, and give thee peace.

Numbers 6:24-26

Mark the perfect man, and behold the upright: for the end of that man is peace.

Psalm 37:37

I will hear what God the Lord will speak: for he will speak peace unto his people, and to his saints . . .

Psalm 85:8

When a man's ways please the Lord, he maketh even his enemies to be at peace with him.

Proverbs 16:7

And the work of righteousness shall be peace; and the effect of righteousness quietness and assurance for ever.
   And my people shall dwell in a peaceable habitation, and in sure dwellings, and in quiet resting places;

Isaiah 32:17,18

For the mountains shall depart, and the hills be removed; but my kindness shall not depart from thee, neither shall the covenant of my peace be removed, saith the Lord that hath mercy on thee.

Isaiah 54:10

For unto us a child is born . . . and his name shall be
called . . . The Prince of Peace.

Isaiah 9:6

Thus saith the Lord, thy Redeemer, the Holy One of Israel;
I am the Lord thy God which teacheth thee to profit,
which leadeth thee by the way that thou shouldest go.
    O that thou hadst hearkened to my commandments!
then had thy peace been as a river, and thy righteousness
as the waves of the sea:
    There is no peace, saith the Lord, unto the wicked.

Isaiah 48:17,18,22

How beautiful upon the mountains are the feet of him
that bringeth good tidings, that publisheth peace. . . that
saith unto Zion, Thy God reigneth!

Isaiah 52:7

(When John the Baptist was born, his father, Zacharias,
was filled with the Holy Ghost, and prophesied, saying, in
part:) And thou, child, shalt be called the prophet of the
Highest: for thou shalt go before the face of the Lord
to prepare his ways;
    To give knowledge of salvation unto his people by the
remission of their sins,
    Through the tender mercy of our God; whereby the
dayspring from on high hath visited us,
    To give light to them that sit in darkness and in the
shadow of death, to guide our feet into the way of peace.

Luke 1:76-79

For the kingdom of God is not meat and drink; but
righteousness, and peace, and joy in the Holy Ghost.
    Let us therefore follow after the things which make
for peace . . .

Romans 14:17,19

. . . the fruit of the Spirit is love, joy, peace, longsuffering,
gentleness, goodness, faith,
    Meekness, temperance . . .

Galatians 5:22,23

93

(When Jesus was born, there were shepherds in the field.)
And, lo, the angel of the Lord came upon them, and the
glory of the Lord shone round about them...

And suddenly there was with the angel a multitude of
the heavenly host praising God, and saying,

Glory to God in the highest, and on earth peace,
good will toward men.

Luke 2:9,13,14

Jesus said: Peace I leave with you, my peace I give unto
you: not as the world giveth, give I unto you. Let not your
heart be troubled, neither let it be afraid.

John 14:27

Jesus said: Salt is good: but if the salt have lost his saltness,
wherewith will ye season it? Have salt in yourselves, and
have peace one with another.

Mark 9:50

Jesus said: These things I have spoken unto you, that in me
ye might have peace. In the world ye shall have tribulation:
but be of good cheer; I have overcome the world.

John 16:33

... to be carnally minded is death; but to be spiritually
minded is life and peace.

Romans 8:6

I therefore, the prisoner of the Lord, beseech you that ye
walk worthy of the vocation wherewith ye are called,

With all lowliness and meekness, with longsuffering,
forbearing one another in love;

Endeavouring to keep the unity of the Spirit in the
bond of peace.

Ephesians 4:1-3

Be careful for nothing; but in every thing by prayer and
supplication with thanksgiving let your requests be made
known unto God.

And the peace of God, which passeth all understanding,
shall keep your hearts and minds through Christ Jesus.

Philippians 4:6,7

. . . Be perfect, be of good comfort, be of one mind, live in peace; and the God of love and peace shall be with you.

2 Corinthians 13:11

. . . at that time ye were without Christ . . . having no hope, and without God in the world:

But now in Christ Jesus ye who sometimes were far off are made nigh by the blood of Christ.

For he is our peace, who hath made both one, and hath broken down the middle wall of partition between us.

Ephesians 2:12-14

And let the peace of God rule in your hearts, to the which also ye are called in one body; and be ye thankful.

Colossians 3:15

. . . the wisdom that is from above is first pure, then peaceable, gentle, and easy to be intreated, full of mercy and good fruits, without partiality, and without hypocrisy.

And the fruit of righteousness is sown in peace of them that make peace.

James 3:17,18

Prayers

Great peace have they which love thy law: and nothing shall offend them.

Psalm 119:165

Thou wilt keep him in perfect peace, whose mind is stayed on thee: because he trusteth in thee.

Isaiah 26:3

I will both lay me down in peace, and sleep: for thou, Lord, only makest me dwell in safety.

Psalm 4:8

Thou Art
My Potter

Thine hands have made me and fashioned me together
round about . . .

    Remember, I beseech thee, that thou hast made me
as the clay . . .

Job 10:8,9

Woe unto them that seek deep to hide their counsel from
the Lord, and their works are in the dark, and they say,
Who seeth us? and who knoweth us?

    Surely your turning of things upside down shall be
esteemed as the potter's clay: for shall the work say of him
that made it, He made me not? or shall the thing framed
say of him that framed it, He had no understanding?

Isaiah 29:15,16

Woe unto him that striveth with his Maker! . . . Shall the
clay say to him that fashioneth it, What makest thou? . . .

Isaiah 45:9

But now, O Lord, thou art our father; we are the clay,
and thou our potter; and we all are the work of thy hand.

Isaiah 64:8

Nay but, O man, who art thou that repliest against God?
Shall the thing formed say to him that formed it, Why hast
thou made me thus?

    Hath not the potter power over the clay . . .

Romans 9:20,21

Have Thine Own Way, Lord, Have Thine Own Way

Have thine own way, Lord! Have thine own way!
Thou art the potter; I am the clay.
Mold me and make me after thy will,
While I am waiting, yielded and still.

Have thine own way, Lord! Have thine own way!
Search me and try me, Master, today!
Whiter than snow, Lord, wash me just now,
As in Thy presence humble I bow.

Have thine own way, Lord! Have thine own way!
Wounded and weary, help me I pray!
Power, all power, surely is thine!
Touch me and heal me, Saviour divine!

Have thine own way, Lord! Have thine own way!
Hold o'er my being absolute sway!
Fill with thy Spirit till all shall see
Christ only, always, living in me!

Adelaide A. Pollard

Prayer

You are my potter, Lord. You alone know the purpose
for which you have created me.

Help me to yield myself willingly and gladly to the
pressure of your hands.

The swift spinning of the potter's wheel of life leaves me
bewildered and confused; enable me, Lord, to relax, and
yield myself to whatever comes, trusting your hands to make
of me the perfect vessel of your own design. Amen.

Thou Art
My Redeemer

Innumerable Bible verses witness to the prevalence of the
idea of God as the Redeemer of His people, both as
individuals and as a nation.

Cruden's Concordance gives two meanings to the word
redeem: (1) To buy again something that has been sold,
by paying back the price to him that bought it . . . (2) To

deliver and bring out of bondage those who were kept
prisoners by their enemies.

Old Testament Selections

Into thine hand I commit my spirit: thou hast redeemed
me, O Lord God of truth.

Psalm 31:5

Hear me, O Lord; for thy lovingkindness is good: turn
unto me according to the multitude of thy tender mercies.
    Draw nigh unto my soul, and redeem it . . .

Psalm 69:16,18

And God spake unto Moses, and said unto him,
I am the Lord:
    Wherefore say unto the children of Israel, I am the Lord,
and I will bring you out from under the burdens of the
Egyptians, and I will rid you out of their bondage, and
I will redeem you with a stretched out arm, and with great
judgments:
    And I will take you to me for a people, and I will be
to you a God . . .

Exodus 6:2,6,7

For I know that my redeemer liveth, and that he shall stand
at the latter day upon the earth.

Job 19:25

But now thus saith the Lord that created thee, O Jacob, and
he that formed thee, O Israel, Fear not: for I have redeemed
thee, I have called thee by thy name; thou art mine.

Isaiah 43:1

I have blotted out, as a thick cloud, thy transgressions,
and, as a cloud, thy sins: return unto me: for I have
redeemed thee.
    Sing, O ye heavens; for the Lord hath done it; shout, ye
lower parts of the earth: break forth into singing, ye

98

mountains, O forest, and every tree therein: for the Lord hath redeemed Jacob, and glorified himself in Israel.

Isaiah 44:22,23

Therefore the redeemed of the Lord shall return, and come with singing unto Zion; and everlasting joy shall be upon their head: they shall obtain gladness and joy; and sorrow and mourning shall flee away.

Isaiah 51:11

I will mention the lovingkindnesses of the Lord, and the praises of the Lord, according to all that the Lord hath bestowed on us, and the great goodness toward the house of Israel, which he hath bestowed on them according to his mercies, and according to the multitude of his lovingkindnesses.

For he said, Surely they are my people, children that will not lie: so he was their Saviour.

In all their affliction he was afflicted, and the angel of his presence saved them: in his love and in his pity he redeemed them; and he bare them, and carried them all the days of old.

Isaiah 63:7-9

In the New Testament

In the New Testament God redeems men or sets them free by something He does in their behalf. The redemption, however, is not by mere announcement; it is an accomplishment of God. A costly act on His part is the means by which He would set men free. The various forms of redemption in the Old Testament always cost something. The Christian redemption is a redemption for which God paid the price. The eternal Father gives from within Himself His eternal Son to redeem men from bondage. Men need to be "set free" from a power greater than themselves, and it is this that God sets Himself to accomplish in Jesus Christ. It cannot be accomplished without cost; but God lays the cost upon Himself, since what the Son endures, the Father also endures, and both endure it from the same motive of holy love. When the means of release is described as a

"ransom" (1 Timothy 2:6, see below) the "cost" to Christ
is implied but in the unique sense of "giving Himself."
A similar self-giving is required of the redeemed: he who
is himself "ransomed" must prepare to be a "ransom."

Madeleine S. Miller
and J. Lane Miller

For there is one God, and one mediator between God and
men, the man Christ Jesus;

Who gave himself a ransom for all, to be testified
in due time.

1 Timothy 2:5,6

Hereby perceive we the love of God, because he laid down
his life for us: and we ought to lay down our lives for the
brethren.

1 John 3:16

For the grace of God that bringeth salvation hath appeared
to all men,

Teaching us that, denying ungodliness and worldly lusts,
we should live soberly, righteously, and godly, in this
present world;

Looking for that blessed hope, and the glorious appearing
of the great God and our Saviour Jesus Christ;

Who gave himself for us, that he might redeem us from
all iniquity, and purify unto himself a peculiar people,
zealous of good works.

Titus 2:11-14

Prayers

How I thank you, O Lord, that you have surely redeemed
me through the life and death and resurrection of your Son,
my Lord and Saviour Jesus Christ.

Give me grace, Father, so to accept your redemptive
love through Jesus, that I may lay hold of your power
to live a truly ransomed life; to be set free from the bondage
of old habits, old attitudes, old bitterness, old sins, and
to enter into the newness of a life completely yielded to your
indwelling Holy Spirit. In Jesus' name. Amen.

Thou Art
My Salvation

Early Hebrews recognized God's power of salvation as innumerable passages attest. It is true that frequently (but not always) the salvation for which they prayed and gave thanks was physical safety from surrounding warlike tribes.

   This section includes Old Testament passages only. The New Testament passages are gathered together in the section "Thou Art My Saviour," and refer almost always to salvation from the consequences of sin.

The Lord liveth; and blessed be my rock; and exalted be the God of the rock of my salvation.

2 Samuel 22:47

For I am the Lord thy God, the Holy One of Israel, thy Saviour . . .
   I, even I, am the Lord; and beside me there is no saviour.

Isaiah 43:3,11

I am the Lord, and there is none else, there is no God beside me . . .

Isaiah 45:5

. . . and all flesh shall know that I the Lord am thy Saviour and thy Redeemer, the mighty One . . .

Isaiah 49:26

Lift up your eyes to the heavens, and look upon the earth beneath: for the heavens shall vanish away like smoke, and the earth shall wax old like a garment, and they that dwell therein shall die in like manner: but my salvation shall be for ever, and my righteousness shall not be abolished.
   Hearken unto me, ye that know righteousness, the people in whose heart is my law; fear ye not the reproach of men, neither be ye afraid of their revilings.
   For the moth shall eat them up like a garment, and the

101

worm shall eat them like wool: but my righteousness shall
be for ever, and my salvation from generation to generation.

Isaiah 51:6-8

The Lord hath made bare his holy arm in the eyes of all
the nations; and all the ends of the earth shall see the
salvation of our God.

Isaiah 52:10

Let all those that seek thee rejoice and be glad in thee:
let such as love thy salvation say continually, The Lord be
magnified.

Psalm 40:16

Behold, the Lord hath proclaimed unto the end of the
world, Say ye to the daughter of Zion, Behold, thy salvation
cometh; behold, his reward is with him . . .
    And they shall call them, The holy people, The redeemed
of the Lord . . .

Isaiah 62:11,12

Truly my soul waiteth upon God: from him cometh my
salvation.
    He only is my rock and my salvation . . .
    My soul, wait thou only upon God; for my expectation
is from him.
    He only is my rock and my salvation: he is my defence;
I shall not be moved.
    In God is my salvation and my glory: the rock of my
strength, and my refuge, is in God.

Psalm 62:1,2,5-7

O sing unto the Lord a new song; for he hath done
marvellous things: his right hand, and his holy arm,
hath gotten him the victory.
    The Lord hath made known his salvation: his
righteousness hath he openly shewed in the sight of the
heathen.
    He hath remembered his mercy and his truth toward
the house of Israel: all the ends of the earth have seen
the salvation of our God.

Psalm 98:1-3

The Lord is righteous in all his ways, and holy in all his works.

The Lord is nigh unto all them that call upon him, to all that call upon him in truth.

He will fulfill the desire of them that fear him: he also will hear their cry, and will save them.

The Lord preserveth all them that love him . . .

Psalm 145:17-20

. . . I the Lord speak righteousness, I declare things that are right.

. . . there is no God else beside me; a just God and a Saviour; there is none beside me.

Look unto me, and be ye saved, all the ends of the earth: for I am God, and there is none else.

Isaiah 45:19,21,22

Strengthen ye the weak hands, and confirm the feeble knees.

Say to them that are of a fearful heart, Be strong, fear not: behold, your God will come . . . he will come and save you.

Isaiah 35:3,4

. . . I am with thee to save thee and to deliver thee, saith the Lord.

Jeremiah 15:20

The Lord thy God in the midst of thee is mighty; he will save, he will rejoice over thee with joy; he will rest in his love, he will joy over thee with singing.

Zephaniah 3:17

Thus saith the Lord of hosts; Behold, I will save my people . . .

And I will bring them, and they shall dwell in the midst of Jerusalem: and they shall be my people, and I will be their God, in truth and in righteousness.

Zechariah 8:7,8

. . . Lo, this is our God; we have waited for him, and he will save us: this is the Lord; we have waited for him, we will be glad and rejoice in his salvation.

Isaiah 25:9

God Is My Strong Salvation

God is my strong salvation:
    What foe have I to fear?
In darkness and temptation,
    My light, my help, is near.

Though hosts encamp around me,
    Firm in the fight I stand;
What terror can confound me,
    With God at my right hand?

Place on the Lord reliance;
    My soul, with courage wait;
His truth be thine affiance,
    When faint and desolate.

His might thy heart shall strengthen,
    His love thy joy increase;
Mercy thy days shall lengthen;
    The Lord will give thee peace.

James Montgomery

Prayers

Save thy people, and bless thine inheritance: feed them
also, and lift them up for ever.

Psalm 28:9

O God, my heart is fixed; I will sing and give praise,
even with my glory.
    I will praise thee, O Lord, among the people. . .
    For thy mercy is great above the heavens: and thy
truth reacheth unto the clouds.
    Be thou exalted, O God, above the heavens: and thy
glory above all the earth.
    . . . save with thy right hand . . .
    Give us help from trouble: for vain is the help of man.

Psalm 108:1,3-6,12

Forsake me not, O Lord: O my God, be not far from me.
    Make haste to help me, O Lord my salvation.

Psalm 38:21,22

Shew us thy mercy, O Lord, and grant us thy salvation.
    Surely his salvation is nigh them that fear him . . .

Psalm 85:7,9

Thou Art
My Saviour

Jesus, Lover of My Soul

Jesus, Lover of my soul,
    Let me to thy bosom fly,
While the nearer waters roll,
    While the tempest still is high:
Hide me, O my Saviour, hide,
    Till the storm of life be past;
Safe into the haven guide,
    O receive my soul at last.

Other refuge have I none,
    Hangs my helpless soul on thee;
Leave, ah! leave me not alone,
    Still support and comfort me!
All my trust on thee is stayed;
    All my help from thee I bring;
Cover my defenceless head
    With the shadow of thy wing.

Plenteous grace with thee is found,
    Grace to cleanse from every sin;
Let the healing streams abound,
    Make and keep me pure within.
Thou of life the fountain art,
    Freely let me take of thee:
Spring thou up within my heart,
    Rise to all eternity.

Charles Wesley

Thou Art My Saviour

Saviour, the term applied to Jesus Christ to express his central significance for mankind . . . The root meaning of the word in the Old Testament is "helper," or "preserver," and this meaning is carried over into the Gospel story in the name given to Jesus. The proper name "Jesus" is the Greek form of the Hebrew word that means "to help," "to preserve," "to save." Jesus therefore bore a name that described his office.

Jesus was to be the Saviour, however, in a very special sense . . . Jesus Christ is Saviour primarily because he brings God and man together in a fellowship of love. This experience, properly understood, affects life in all its aspects: it has had an incalculable influence on civilization. The saving work of Christ has brought a new conception of personality and of its rich possibilities . . . It has created in the world a new social sense . . . He came into the world expressly to save it; he could save it because he was the Son of God in the flesh; and the root and center of the salvation is a "personal experience" which in its turn is the promise of both that perfect conformity to the will of God which is the purpose of man's existence, and of that relation to other men which is essential to the realized family of God.

Madeleine S. Miller
and J. Lane Miller

Now the birth of Jesus Christ was on this wise: When as his mother Mary was espoused to Joseph, before they came together, she was found with child of the Holy Ghost.

Then Joseph her husband, being a just man, and not willing to make her a publick example, was minded to put her away privily.

But while he thought on these things, behold, the angel of the Lord appeared unto him in a dream, saying, Joseph, thou son of David, fear not to take unto thee Mary thy wife: for that which is conceived in her is of the Holy Ghost.

And she shall bring forth a son, and thou shalt call his name JESUS: for he shall save his people from their sins.

Matthew 1:18-21

For God so loved the world, that he gave his only begotten
Son, that whosoever believeth in him should not perish,
but have everlasting life.

For God sent not his Son into the world to condemn the
world; but that the world through him might be saved.

John 3:16,17

Other passages in the New Testament confirm Jesus' right
to the title "Saviour." In the story of the Samaritan woman
at the well, when she had returned to the village and brought
back a number of people to hear Jesus, many believed
on him.

And (they) said unto the woman, Now we believe, not
because of thy saying: for we have heard him ourselves,
and know that this is indeed the Christ, the Saviour of
the world.

John 4:42

Then there is the familiar incident toward the end of Jesus'
life, when he and his disciples were journeying to Jerusalem
for the last time, when the people in a Samaritan village
refused to receive them.

And when his disciples James and John saw this, they said,
Lord, wilt thou that we command fire to come down from
heaven, and consume them, even as Elias did?

But he turned, and rebuked them, and said, Ye know
not what manner of spirit ye are of.

For the Son of man is not come to destroy men's lives,
but to save them . . .

Luke 9:54-56

Jesus said: Take heed that ye despise not one of these
little ones . . .

For the Son of man is come to save that which was lost.

How think ye? if a man have an hundred sheep, and
one of them be gone astray, doth he not leave the ninety
and nine, and goeth into the mountains, and seeketh that
which is gone astray?

And if so be that he find it, verily I say unto you, he

rejoiceth more of that sheep, than of the ninety and nine
which went not astray.

Even so it is not the will of your Father which is in
heaven, that one of these little ones should perish.

In Acts 5, the apostles witnessed to the high priest and
to the council, in these words:

The God of our fathers raised up Jesus, whom ye slew
and hanged on a tree.

Him hath God exalted with his right hand to be a
Prince and a Saviour, for to give repentance to Israel, and
forgiveness of sins.

And we are his witnesses of these things . . .

Acts 5:30-32

(Paul writes) This is a faithful saying, and worthy of all
acceptation, that Christ Jesus came into the world to save
sinners; of whom I am chief.

1 Timothy 1:15

Be not thou therefore ashamed of the testimony of our
Lord, nor of me his prisoner: but be thou partaker of the
afflictions of the gospel according to the power of God;

Who hath saved us, and called us with an holy calling,
not according to our works, but according to his own
purpose and grace, which was given us in Christ Jesus
before the world began,

But is now made manifest by the appearing of our
Saviour Jesus Christ, who hath abolished death, and hath
brought life and immortality to light through the gospel.

2 Timothy 1:8-10

For we ourselves also were sometimes foolish, disobedient,
deceived, serving divers lusts and pleasures, living in malice
and envy, hateful, and hating one another.

But after that the kindness and love of God our Saviour
toward man appeared,

Not by works of righteousness which we have done, but
according to his mercy he saved us, by the washing of
regeneration, and renewing of the Holy Ghost;

Which he shed on us abundantly through Jesus Christ our Saviour;

That being justified by his grace, we should be made heirs according to the hope of eternal life.

Titus 3:3-7

. . . grow in grace, and in the knowledge of our Lord and Saviour Jesus Christ. To him be glory both now and for ever. Amen.

2 Peter 3:18

In this was manifested the love of God toward us, because that God sent his only begotten Son into the world, that we might live through him.

Herein is love, not that we loved God, but that he loved us, and sent his Son to be the propitiation for our sins.

Beloved, if God so loved us, we ought also to love one another.

No man hath seen God at any time. If we love one another, God dwelleth in us, and his love is perfected in us.

Hereby know we that we dwell in him, and he in us, because he hath given us of his Spirit.

And we have seen and do testify that the Father sent the Son to be the Saviour of the world.

1 John 4:9-14

Now unto him that is able to keep you from falling, and to present you faultless before the presence of his glory with exceeding joy,

To the only wise God our Saviour, be glory and majesty, dominion and power, both now and ever. Amen.

Jude 24,25

Savior, Thy Dying Love

Savior, thy dying love
    Thou gavest me,
Nor should I aught withhold,
    Dear Lord, from thee;
In love my soul would bow,
My heart fulfill its vow,
Some offering bring thee now,
    Something for thee.

Give me a faithful heart,
    Likeness to thee,
That each departing day
    Henceforth may see
Some work of love begun,
Some deed of kindness done,
Some wanderer sought and won,
    Something for thee.

All that I am and have,
    Thy gifts so free,
In joy, in grief, through life,
    Dear Lord, for thee;
And when thy face I see
My ransomed soul shall be,
Through all eternity,
    Something for thee.

Sylvanus Dryden Phelps

110

Thou Art
My Shepherd

Saviour, Like a Shepherd Lead Us

Saviour, like a shepherd lead us,
　　Much we need thy tender care;
In thy pleasant pastures feed us;
　　For our use thy folds prepare:
　　　　Blessèd Jesus!
　　Thou hast bought us, thine we are.

Early let us seek thy favor,
　　Early let us learn thy will;
Do thou, Lord, our only Saviour,
　　With thy love our bosoms fill:
　　　　Blessèd Jesus!
　　Thou hast loved us: love us still.

D. A. Thrupp

Thou Art My Shepherd

Behold, the Lord God will come with strong hand,
and his arm shall rule for him . . .
　　He shall feed his flock like a shepherd: he shall gather
the lambs with his arm, and carry them in his bosom, and
shall gently lead those that are with young.

Isaiah 40:10,11

For thus saith the Lord God; Behold, I, even I, will both
search my sheep, and seek them out.
　　As a shepherd seeketh out his flock in the day that he is
among his sheep that are scattered; so will I seek out my
sheep, and will deliver them out of all places where they
have been scattered in the cloudy and dark day.
　　I will feed my flock, and I will cause them to lie down,
saith the Lord God.

I will seek that which was lost, and bring again that
which was driven away, and will bind up that which was
broken, and will strengthen that which was sick . . .

Ezekiel 34:11,12,15,16

O come, let us worship and bow down: let us kneel before
the Lord our maker.

For he is our God; and we are the people of his pasture,
and the sheep of his hand . . .

Psalm 95:6,7

Make a joyful noise unto the Lord, all ye lands.

Serve the Lord with gladness: come before his presence
with singing.

Know ye that the Lord he is God: it is he that hath made
us, and not we ourselves; we are his people, and the sheep
of his pasture.

Psalm 100:1-3

Jesus said: I am the good shepherd: the good shepherd
giveth his life for the sheep.

I am the good shepherd, and know my sheep, and am
known of mine.

And other sheep I have, which are not of this fold:
them also I must bring, and they shall hear my voice;
and there shall be one fold, and one shepherd.

John 10:11,14,16

In Heavenly Love Abiding

In heavenly love abiding,
    No change my heart shall fear,
And safe is such confiding,
    For nothing changes here.
The storm may roar without me,
    My heart may low be laid;
But God is round about me,
    And can I be dismayed?

Wherever he may guide me,
    No want shall turn me back;
My shepherd is beside me,
    And nothing can I lack.
His wisdom ever waketh,
    His sight is never dim;
He knows the way he taketh,
    And I will walk with him.

Green pastures are before me,
    Which yet I have not seen;
Bright skies will soon be o'er me,
    Where the dark clouds have been.
My hope I cannot measure,
    The path to life is free;
My Saviour has my treasure,
    And he will walk with me.

Anna L. Waring

So we thy people and sheep of thy pasture will give thee
thanks for ever: we will shew forth thy praise to all
generations.

Psalm 79:13

The Shepherd Psalm

Thou art my shepherd, Lord;
    I shall not want.
    Thou makest me to lie down
    in green pastures;
    thou leadest me beside the still waters.
    Thou restorest my soul;
    thou leadest me in the paths
    of righteousness for thy name's sake.
Yea, though I walk through the valley
    of the shadow of death,
    I will fear no evil:
    for thou art with me;
    thy rod and thy staff they comfort me.
Thou preparest a table before me
    in the presence of mine enemies:
    thou anointest my head with oil;
    my cup runneth over.
Surely goodness and mercy
    shall follow me
    all the days of my life;
    and I will dwell in thy house,
    O Lord, for ever. Amen.

Saviour, Teach Me, Day by Day

Saviour, teach me, day by day,
Thine own lesson to obey;
Better lesson cannot be,
Loving him who first loved me.

With a childlike heart of love,
At thy bidding may I move;
Prompt to serve and follow thee,
Loving him who first loved me.

Teach me all thy steps to trace,
Strong to follow in thy grace;
Learning how to live from thee;
Loving him who first loved me. Amen.

J. E. Leeson

Thou Art
My Shield

Thou Art My Shield

Many there be which say of my soul, There is no help
for him in God.

 But thou, O Lord, art a shield for me; my glory, and
the lifter up of mine head.

 I cried unto the Lord with my voice, and he heard me
out of his holy hill.

 I will not be afraid of ten thousands of people, that have
set themselves against me round about.

Psalm 3:2-4,6

. . . Fear not . . . I am thy shield, and thy exceeding
great reward.

Genesis 15:1

For the Lord God is a sun and shield: the Lord will give
grace and glory: no good thing will he withhold from them
that walk uprightly.

Psalm 84:11

Our soul waiteth for the Lord: he is our help and our shield.
 For our heart shall rejoice in him, because we have
trusted in his holy name.

Psalm 33:20,21

The Lord is my strength and my shield; my heart trusted
in him, and I am helped: therefore my heart greatly
rejoiceth; and with my song will I praise him.

Psalm 28:7

Every word of God is pure: he is a shield unto them that
put their trust in him.

Proverbs 30:5

In the Hour of Trial

In the hour of trial,
    Jesus, plead for me,
Lest by base denial
    I depart from thee.
When thou seest me waver,
    With a look recall,
Nor for fear or favor
    Suffer me to fall.

With forbidden pleasures
    Would this vain world charm,
Or its sordid treasures
    Spread to work me harm,
Bring to my remembrance
    Sad Gethsemane,
Or, in darker semblance
    Cross-crowned Calvary.

Should thy mercy send me
    Sorrow, toil or woe,
Or should pain attend me
    On my path below,
Grant that I may never
    Fail thy hand to see;
Grant that I may ever
    Cast my care on thee.

James Montgomery

Prayers

For thou, Lord, wilt bless the righteous; with favour wilt
thou compass him as with a shield.

Psalm 5:12

Thou hast also given me the shield of thy salvation:
and thy gentleness hath made me great.

2 Samuel 22:36

Thou art my hiding place and my shield . . .

Psalm 119:114

Help me to realize, Holy Father, that you are in very truth my shield: that nothing comes to me in the daily struggle of life save that which is part of your will for me.

You are my shield — protecting me from trials and tribulations too difficult for me to handle; keeping from me temptations beyond my strength to resist.

Increase in me, I pray, courage and strength, and give me the comforting assurance of your constantly surrounding love and protection.

In the name of your Son, my Lord and Saviour, Jesus Christ. Amen.

Thou Art
My Strength

Thou Art My Strength

God is my strength and power: and he maketh my way perfect.

He maketh my feet like hinds' feet: and setteth me upon my high places.

Thou hast enlarged my steps under me; so that my feet did not slip.

2 Samuel 22:33,34,37

The Lord is my strength and my shield; my heart trusted in him, and I am helped: therefore my heart greatly rejoiceth; and with my song will I praise him.

The Lord is . . . the saving strength of his anointed.

Psalm 28:7,8

Be strong and of a good courage, fear not, nor be afraid . . .
for the Lord thy God, he it is that doth go with thee;
he will not fail thee, nor forsake thee.

Deuteronomy 31:6

My Faith Looks Up to Thee

My faith looks up to thee,
Thou Lamb of Calvary,
    Saviour divine!
Now hear me while I pray;
Take all my guilt away;
O let me from this day
    Be wholly thine.

May thy rich grace impart
Strength to my fainting heart,
    My zeal inspire;
As thou hast died for me,
O, may my love to thee
Pure, warm, and changeless be,
    A living fire.

While life's dark maze I tread,
And griefs around me spread,
    Be thou my guide;
Bid darkness turn to day;
Wipe sorrow's tears away;
Nor let me ever stray
    From thee aside.

When ends life's transient dream,
When death's cold, sullen stream
    Shall o'er me roll;
Blest Saviour, then in love,
Fear and distrust remove;
O, bear me safe above,
    A ransomed soul.

Ray Palmer

Prayers

. . . be not thou far from me, O Lord: O my strength, haste thee to help me.

Psalm 22:19

O Lord God of hosts, who is a strong Lord like unto thee? . . .
    Thou hast a mighty arm: strong is thy hand . . .

Psalm 89:8,13

I will praise thee with my whole heart . . .
    In the day when I cried thou answeredst me, and strengthenedst me with strength in my soul.
    . . . thy mercy, O Lord, endureth for ever . . .

Psalm 138:1,3,8

I will love thee, O Lord, my strength.

Psalm 18:1

. . . Now therefore, O God, strengthen my hands.

Nehemiah 6:9

Hear my cry, O God; attend unto my prayer.

From the end of the earth will I cry unto thee, when my heart is overwhelmed: lead me to the rock that is higher than I.

For thou hast been a shelter for me, and a strong tower from the enemy.

I will abide in thy tabernacle for ever: I will trust in the covert of thy wings.

Psalm 61:1-4

Thou Art
My Teacher

Thou Art My Teacher

Out of heaven he made thee to hear his voice, that he might instruct thee . . .

Deuteronomy 4:36

Good and upright is the Lord: therefore will he teach sinners in the way.

The meek will he guide in judgment: and the meek will he teach his way.

Psalm 25:8,9

Yet they say, The Lord shall not see, neither shall the God of Jacob regard it.

Understand, ye brutish among the people: and ye fools, when will ye be wise?

He that planted the ear, shall he not hear? he that formed the eye, shall he not see?

. . . he that teacheth man knowledge, shall he not know?

Psalm 94:7-10

Behold, God exalteth by his power: who teacheth like him?

Job 36:22

120

Spirit of God, Descend Upon My Heart

Spirit of God, descend upon my heart;
    Wean it from earth, through all its pulses move;
Stoop to my weakness, mighty as thou art,
    And make me love thee as I ought to love.

I ask no dream, no prophet ecstasies,
    No sudden rending of the veil of clay,
No angel visitant, no opening skies,
    But take the dimness of my soul away.

Hast thou not bid me love thee, God and King?
    All, all thine own, soul, heart, and strength and mind?
I see thy cross; there teach my heart to cling;
    O let me seek thee, and O let me find!

Teach me to feel that thou are always nigh;
    Teach me the struggles of the soul to bear,
To check the rising doubt, the rebel sigh;
    Teach me the patience of unanswered prayer.

Teach me to love thee as thine angels love,
    One holy passion filling all my frame;
The baptism of the heaven-descended Dove,
    My heart an altar, and thy love the flame. Amen.

George Croly

Prayers

Thy testimonies are wonderful: therefore doth my soul
keep them.
  The entrance of thy words giveth light; it giveth
understanding unto the simple.
  Order my steps in thy word: and let not any iniquity
have dominion over me.
  Make thy face to shine upon thy servant; and teach me
thy statutes.

Psalm 119:129,130,133,135

Shew me thy ways, O Lord; teach me thy paths.

Lead me in thy truth, and teach me: for thou art the God of my salvation; on thee do I wait all the day.

Psalm 25:4,5

Teach me thy way, O Lord, and lead me in a plain path . . .

Psalm 27:11

Teach me thy way, O Lord; I will walk in thy truth: unite my heart to fear thy name.

I will praise thee, O Lord my God, with all my heart: and I will glorify thy name for evermore.

Psalm 86:11,12

Teach me, O Lord, the way of thy statutes; and I shall keep it unto the end.

Give me understanding, and I shall keep thy law; yea, I shall observe it with my whole heart.

Make me to go in the path of thy commandments; for therein do I delight.

Psalm 119:33-35

Thou hast dealt well with thy servant, O Lord, according unto thy word.

Teach me good judgment and knowledge: for I have believed thy commandments.

Before I was afflicted I went astray: but now have I kept thy word.

Thou art good, and doest good; teach me thy statutes.

Psalm 119:65-68

And many people shall go and say, Come ye, and let us go up to the mountain of the Lord, to the house of the God of Jacob; and he will teach us of his ways, and we will walk in his paths . . .

Isaiah 2:3

But in the last days it shall come to pass, that the mountain of the house of the Lord shall be established in the top of the mountains, and it shall be exalted above the hills; and people shall flow unto it.

And many nations shall come, and say, Come, and let us

go up to the mountain of the Lord, and to the house of the
God of Jacob; and he will teach us of his ways, and we will
walk in his paths: for the law shall go forth of Zion, and
the word of the Lord from Jerusalem.

And he shall judge among many people, and rebuke
strong nations afar off; and they shall beat their swords into
plowshares, and their spears into pruninghooks: nation
shall not lift up a sword against nation, neither shall they
learn war any more.

But they shall sit every man under his vine and under
his fig tree; and none shall make them afraid: for the mouth
of the Lord of hosts hath spoken it.

Micah 4:1-4

Amen, Lord, so be it!

Thou Art
My Victory

Thou Art My Victory

As I was planning this book and working on its early
chapters, I realized one day that of course the climaxing and
concluding chapter of it must be "Thou Art My Victory!"
When, however, I came to search the *Concordance* for
"victorious" passages, I was disappointed. The references
were few and far between. I tried to think of synonyms,
and came up with "triumph" — and that added a few more,
but still I was not satisfied.

And then one day when I was not even thinking about
the book, in reading in Revelation, I suddenly came across
(or was led to!) the phrase "to him that overcometh."
Of course! There it was! I knew it must be somewhere.
I was reminded of a chorus we often sing at church:

By the Word of the Lord
We are made overcomers,
By the Word of the Lord
We are able to stand.

I picked up my pen and note-book, and searched through the Book of Revelation with an exciting sense of discovery — for there, one after another, I found God's glorious promises to "him that overcometh."

Now of course, in Revelation these promises are made to that blessed host, beginning with Stephen, those whose spectacular victory over the forces of evil in the world had been won in the face of unimaginable persecution and physical suffering. But God's promises are not limited. The words He spoke to Jacob (for instance): "Lo, I am with thee and will keep thee in all places whither thou goest" — He still speaks over and over to individuals in every generation. So, too, the promises in the Book of Revelation are also spoken to us today, when we become "overcomers", when in the strength of our living Lord we are able to live triumphantly amid the trials and tribulations of our lives. Admittedly, the circumstances we have to overcome are seldom as formidable as those the martyrs of the first generation of Christians endured; nevertheless, no one of us escapes the dark valleys of suffering (physical and spiritual), and the black nights of despair that test our courage and our faith. And these promises are for us, too.

He that hath an ear, let him hear what the Spirit saith unto the churches; To him that overcometh will I give to eat of the tree of life, which is in the midst of the paradise of God.

Revelation 2:7

Dr. Lynn Harold Hough says of this verse:

The Genesis story tells of a tree the fruit of which was forbidden. The message to the Ephesians tells of a tree of life of which Christian victors are allowed to eat. After trial comes satisfaction. There are some things which can be given safely to men only after they have been disciplined and, through firmness under the pressures of life, have attained genuine strength . . . The Christian desires to meet

124

the conditions for eating of the tree of life. That tree suggests noble discipline.

He that hath an ear, let him hear what the Spirit saith unto the churches; He that overcometh shall not be hurt of the second death.

Revelation 2:11

. . . To him that overcometh will I give to eat of the hidden manna, and will give him a white stone, and in the stone a new name written, which no man knoweth saving he that receiveth it.

Revelation 2:17

Dr. Hough sees in this promise "The Secret Glory of the Individual life," and adds these helpful comments:

When Christianity is interpreted as a corporate experience it is easy to forget its significance as an individual experience. When we think of the Christian victory in social relations it is possible to forget its deep and mighty victory in the individual life. The classical passage in the New Testament about the individual is the promise of the *white stone,* with a new name written on *the stone which no one knows except him who receives it.* Each victorious Christian is to have an eternal secret with God. There is a central citadel in each personality which only God shares. God completely cleanses a man's life. So the stone he gives him is a *white stone.* The *new name* represents the individual personality achieved only through the grace of Christ. He is a new man, but he is not a new man just like every other new man. He is eternally something individual, and different, and eternally prized by God.

He that overcometh, the same shall be clothed in white raiment; and I will not blot out his name out of the book of life but I will confess his name before my Father, and before his angels.

Revelation 3:5

"White raiment" is the symbol of righteousness and immortality. Dr. Hough comments:

125

It might seem that nothing is less possible than to walk
through this world without soiling one's garments. But . . .
how often we meet in churches everywhere people whose
sheer goodness — a goodness of which they themselves
are entirely unconscious — gives happiness and moral
reassurance to all who know them . . . In rare and beautiful
books we have met these great Christians. Best of all we
have met them moving simply and quietly through the life
of seemingly very ordinary churches.

Him that overcometh will I make a pillar in the temple of
my God, and he shall go no more out . . .

Revelation 3:12

In the temple built of souls, the Christian person is an
essential support.

Dr. Lynn Harold Hough

To him that overcometh will I grant to sit with me in my
throne, even as I also overcame, and am set down with
my Father in his throne.

Revelation 3:21

The boundless generosity of the promises made to the man
who is victorious through Christ flashes out in the amazing
word, *I will grant him to sit with me on my throne.* There
is not only felicity, there is authority and power. Christ . . .
shares his throne with him who conquers. The limitless
power of the divine grace is suggested by these words . . .
The picture of Christ sharing his throne surpasses all other
symbols of Christian hope.

Dr. Lynn Harold Hough

He that overcometh shall inherit all things; and I will be
his God, and he shall be my son.

Revelation 21:7

This is the final and all-inclusive promise, the glorious and
complete fulfillment, the summation of all that the victor's
crown assures.

Thou art our God — we are Thy children.

Additional New Testament Selections

Jesus said: Behold, the hour cometh, yea, is now come, that
ye shall be scattered, every man to his own, and shall leave
me alone: and yet I am not alone, because the Father
is with me.

These things I have spoken unto you, that in me ye
might have peace. In the world ye shall have tribulation:
but be of good cheer; I have overcome the world.

John 16 :32,33

Be not overcome of evil, but overcome evil with good.

Romans 12:21

. . . greater is he that is in you, than he that is in the world.

1 John 4:4

For this corruptible must put on incorruption, and this
mortal must put on immortality.

So when this corruptible shall have put on incorruption,
and this mortal shall have put on immortality, then shall
be brought to pass the saying that is written, Death is
swallowed up in victory.

O death, where is thy sting? O grave, where is thy
victory?

The sting of death is sin; and the strength of sin is
the law.

But thanks be to God, which giveth us the victory
through our Lord Jesus Christ.

1 Corinthians 15:53-57

Whosoever believeth that Jesus is the Christ is born
of God. . .

For whatsoever is born of God overcometh the world:
and this is the victory that overcometh the world, even
our faith.

1 John 5:1,4

Now thanks be unto God, which always causeth us to
triumph in Christ . . .

2 Corinthians 2:14

I Heard an Old, Old Story

I heard an old, old story,
How a Saviour came from glory,
How He gave His life on Calvary
To save a wretch like me;
I heard about His groaning,
Of His precious blood's atoning,
Then I repented of my sins
And won the victory.

I heard about His healing,
Of His cleansing power revealing,
How he made the lame to walk again
And caused the blind to see;
And then I cried "Dear Jesus,
Come and heal my broken spirit,"
And somehow Jesus came and brought
To me the victory.

I heard about a mansion
He has built for me in glory,
And I heard about the streets of gold
Beyond the crystal sea;
About the angels singing,
And the old redemption story,
And some sweet day I'll sing up there
The song of victory.

Refrain:
    O victory in Jesus,
    My Saviour, for ever,
        He sought me and bought me
    With his redeeming blood;
    He loved me ere I knew Him
    And all my love is due Him,
    He plunged me to victory
    Beneath the cleansing flood.

Eugene M. Bartlett

Prayers

Unto thee, O Lord, do I lift up my soul.
    O my God, I trust in thee: let me not be ashamed,
let not mine enemies triumph over me.

Psalm 25:1,2

Thine, O Lord, is the greatness, and the power, and the
glory, and the victory, and the majesty: for all that is in
the heaven and in the earth is thine; thine is the kingdom,
O Lord, and thou art exalted as head above all.
    Both riches and honour come of thee, and thou reignest
over all; and in thine hand is power and might; and in thine
hand it is to make great, and to give strength unto all.
    Now therefore, our God, we thank thee, and praise thy
glorious name.

1 Chronicles 29:11-13

My Prayer for Myself
and for Those Who May Read This Book

Father, grant to us

That Christ may dwell in our hearts
        by faith; that we, being rooted
        and grounded in love,

May be able to comprehend with all
        saints, what is the breadth, and
        length, and depth, and height;

And to know the love of Christ,
        which passeth knowledge, that we
        might be filled with all the
        fulness of God.

Now unto him that is able to do
        exceeding abundantly above
        all that we ask or think,
        according to the power that
        worketh in us,

Unto him be glory in the church by
Christ Jesus throughout all ages,
world without end. Amen.

Ephesians 3:17-20

A Final Word

At a recent conference, Iverna Tompkins was leading a group in a study of "Worship." In one session she pointed out the many different ways in which we relate to God; and the following meditation includes many of the ideas she expressed. I am grateful to her for permission to include them here.

Receivers

When we relate to God as our *Creator,* we come to Him as His creatures, the work of His hands, recognizing our very being as His gift to us.

When we relate to Him as our *Comforter,* we come in our deepest griefs; receiving from Him the indescribable gift of His understanding and tender compassion.

When we relate to Him as our *Defender,* we come in utter helplessness; receiving from Him assurance of His available strength, and unfailing protection.

When we relate to Him as our *Deliverer,* we come to Him as captives, bound in the chains of old habits, old sins, false teachings; and we receive from Him the breaking of our fetters.

When we relate to Him as our *Guide,* we come as lost and bewildered pilgrims on life's journey; and we receive from Him clear and specific guidance for our daily walk.

When we relate to Him as our *Healer,* we come broken in
body, mind and spirit; and we receive restoration
and renewal.

When we relate to Him as our *Helper,* we come in full
awareness of our weakness, failures and inadequacies;
and we discover that He is in truth "a very present
help in trouble."

When we relate to Him as our *Redeemer,* we come
recognizing that we are not our own, we have been
bought with a price.

When we relate to Him as our *Shepherd,* we come as
sheep, content to follow where He leads, trusting
His provision for our every need.

When we relate to Him as our *Saviour,* we come as guilt-
laden sinners, repentant; and we receive His full and
free forgiveness.

In all of these relationships we are *receivers only* — until
our hearts are deeply stirred, and our whole being offers
up joyous thanksgiving to God. Then we begin to worship.
But this is only the first step in genuine worship — it is
still self-centered, praising God for what He has done
for *me.*

Givers

As we draw closer to God, and allow His indwelling
Spirit to guide us into deeper truth, we discover areas of
relationship with God in which we may become *givers*
as well as receivers.

When we relate to God as our *Father,* when we come to
Him, not as feeble newborn babes, but as mature
sons and daughters, eager and willing to be
dedicated and obedient fellow-workers with Him

wherever He may use us, then we are giving Him
the deep desire of His heart — the genuine fellowship
for which He created us.

When we relate to *Jesus Christ* as our *Lord* and *Master,*
we come as servants, offering Him our lives as
"living sacrifices" to use for His eternal purposes.

When we relate to God the *Holy Spirit* in-dwelling us, we
discover Him as the Revealer of truth we need to
know, as the "still, small voice" of conscience, as the
Enabler by whom we are strengthened to yield
ourselves in complete and unquestioning obedience.

Thou art our God — the triune God, Father, Son and
Holy Spirit — omnipresent, omniscient, omnipotent!
We come to You as worshippers, filled with awe
before mysteries far beyond our human understanding;
and we lift our hands and hearts in joyous praise
and adoration.

Holy! Holy! Holy!
We praise You, Father,
We love You,
We worship You,
We acknowledge You as Lord of all!
Praise Your holy name, God,
Praise Your holy name!
Hallelujah! Hallelujah!
Hallelujah! Amen.

Index to Biblical Quotations

Genesis
1:26,27 19
2:7 78
15:1 115
28:13,15 67

Exodus
6:2,6,7 98
15:11,13 46

Numbers
6:24-26 . . . . . . 68, 92

Deuteronomy
4:36 120
30:15,16,19,20 79
31:6 118

1 Samuel
2:2,7-9 67

2 Samuel
22:33,34,37 117
22:36 116
22:47 101

1 Chronicles
16:10 61
16:31 61
28:9 13
28:20 11
29:11-13 129

2 Chronicles
7:14 47
32:7,8 51

Nehemiah
6:9 119
8:10 62

Job
10:8,9 96
19:25 98
33:4 79
36:22 120

Psalms
3:2-4,6 115
4:6 88
4:7 63
4:8 95
5:11 . . . . 26, 66

5:12 116
7:10 24
8:1,3-9 23
9:1,2 65
10:14 35
15:1,2,5 32
16:8,9 64
16:11 66
18:1,2 . . . . . . 43, 119
18:28 83
20:1,2,6-8 24
22:19 . . . . . . 53, 119
22:27,28 73
23 (alt.) 114
23:6 30
24:1,7-10 72
25:1,2 129
25:4,5 122
25:8,9 120
25:20 68
27:1 84
27:4,5 30
27:8-10 54
27:11 122
27:14 25
28:7 115
28:7,8 117
28:9 104
29:1,2,10,11 73
30:2 48
30:4,5 61
30:10 53
30:11,12 . . . . . . 18, 66
31:1,2 30
31:1-4 26
31:1,3 46
31:5 98
31:7 66
31:14,15,19,20 13
31:19,20 69
31:23,24 54
32:7 29
32:8,9 45
32:11 61
33:1 61
33:18 11
33:20,21 . . . . . . 52, 115
33:22 58
34:1,3,4 28
35:9 64
36:5,7,9 81
37:37 92
37:39,40 . . . . . . 27, 52

38:15 58
38:21,22 . . . . . . 53, 104
40:16 102
42:5 52
42:11 . . . . 48, 54
43:3 88
44:4 76
46:1-3 52
47:1,2,6-8 72
48:1,14 44
50:1,2 84
50:7,15 27
54:4 51
59:9 25
59:16,17 26
61:1-4 120
62:1,2,5-7 102
63:1,3,5-7 53
64:10 60
67:1 84
67:1,2 47
68:3,4 62
68:5 35
69:16,18 98
70:5 29
71:3 33
71:1,3 43
71:1,4,5,8,12,14,19 . . . 58
73:23,24 46
78:2-7 57
79:8,9 53
79:13 113
80:3 88
84:11 115
85:8 92
85:7,9 104
86:11,12 122
89:8,13 119
90:1,2 33
90:14,15 65
91:1,9,10 30
91:14-16 27
91:2 43
94:7-10 120
94:22 25
95:1-7 73
95:6,7 112
96:11-13 62
97:1,6,11,12 61
98:1-3 102
98:4 61
100:1,2 61
100:1-3 112

103:1-3 47
103:13 35
104:33,34 63
105:1-3 62
108:1,3-6,12 104
116:1-6 27
116:8,17 29
118:24 63
118:28 13
118:29 11
119:33-35 122
119:65-68 122
119:73 22
119:114 117
119:129,130,133,135 . . . 121
119:165 95
121:1-3 51
121:4-8 67
123:2 88
124:7,8 52
125:1,2 30
126:3 64
130:7,8 55
138:1,3,8 119
139:1-4,6,23,24 23
139:14-17 81
143:8-10 29
144:1,2 43
145:1,2,5,6,10,11,13,15,16 . . 76
145:17-20 103
146:5 55
148 20

Proverbs
3:11,12 35
10:28 55
12:28 79
14:26,27 79
16:7 92
24:12 67
30:5 115

Ecclesiastes
11:5 20
12:1,6,7,13,14 21

Isaiah
2:3 122
2:5 84
6:1,5 71
9:2 84
9:6 93
25:1,4 13
25:9 103
26:3 . . . . 69, 95
29:15,16 96

32:17,18 92
35:3,4 103
35:10 60
40:10,11 111
40:28,29,31 13
41:10,13 53
43:1 98
43:2,3 11
43:3,11 101
43:14,15,25 72
44:22,23 98
45:5 101
45:9 96
45:19,21,22 103
48:17,18,22 93
49:13-15 35
49:26 101
50:7 52
51:3 . . . . 16, 60
51:6-8 101
51:11 99
51:12,13 16
52:7 93
52:9 17
52:10 102
53:4,5 48
54:10 . . . . 11, 92
55:6,7 11
55:12 60
57:15,20,21 31
58:6-11 45
60:1,19 84
61:1-3 16
61:10,11 65
62:11,12 102
63:7-9 99
64:8 96
65:17,18 60

Jeremiah
10:6,7,10,12 73
15:20 103
16:19 43
17:7 55
17:13,14,17 58
17:14 48
29:13 11
31:8,9 35
50:6,7 55

Lamentations
3:22-26 55

Ezekiel
34:11,12,15,16 112

Daniel
4:3 74

Joel
2:23 62
3:14-16 56

Amos
4:13 20

Micah
4:1-4 123
7:8,9 84

Habakkuk
3:17-19 . . . . . . 18, 64

Zephaniah
3:17 103

Zechariah
8:7,8 103

Malachi
1:6 89
2:10 35

Matthew
1:18-21 106
4:23 49
5:10-12 62
5:14,16 36
5:43-45 36
6:5-8 36
6:13 29
6:9-13 40
6:10 77
6:25,26,28-33 37
7:7-11 37
7:21 37
10:1,5,7,8 49
10:16,22,24,25,27-29,31 . . . 89
12:15 48
13:31-33 75
13:44-46 75
14:14 49
18:10-14 107
23:1-8,10-12 89

Mark
9:50 94

Luke
1:76-79 93
2:9,13,14 94

4:18	28
4:18,19	48
9:54-56	107
10:1	50
12:29-31	75
15:11-24	37

John

1:1,4	79
1:1-5,14	84
3:16,17	107
3:19-21	85
3:36	79
4:42	107
5:24	79
5:39,40	79
6:33,35,40	80
8:12	85
9:5	85
10:11,14,16	112
11:25,26	80
12:44-46	85
13:3-5,12-17	90
14:6	80
14:15-18	16
14:27	94
15:4,5	31
15:9-11	63
16:32,33	127
16:33	94
17:11-15,20-23	68
20:30,31	80

Acts

5:12,15,16	49
5:30-32	108
17:24-28	80

Romans

5:1-5	56
6:3,4	81
7:18,19,24,25	28
8:6	94
8:14-16	38
8:24,25,28	56
9:20,21	96
12:21	127
14:17	63

14:17,19	93
15:13	57, 66

1 Corinthians

15:53-57	127

2 Corinthians

1:3,4	18
2:14	127
4:5,6	86
13:11	95

Galatians

2:20	81
5:22,23	93

Ephesians

1:15-20	56
2:8-10	21
2:12-14	95
3:17-20	130
4:1-3	94
4:4-6	39
5:8	85

Philippians

4:4	63
4:6,7	94

Colossians

1:9-13 (alt.)	29
3:1-3	81
3:15	95

1 Thessalonians

5:8	58
5:16	63

2 Thessalonians

2:16,17	58
3:3	67

1 Timothy

1:1,2	55
1:15	108
1:17	72
2:5,6	100

2 Timothy

1:8-10	108

Titus

2:11-14	57, 100
3:3-7	108

Hebrews

13:5,6	52

James

3:17,18	95

1 Peter

1:3,8	66
2:9,10	86
4:12,13	63

2 Peter

3:18	109

1 John

1:5-7	86
2:3-6	31
2:8-11	86
3:1,2	39
3:16	100
4:4	127
4:9-14	109
4:13,15,16	31
5:1,4	127

Jude

24,25	66, 109

Revelation

2:7	124
2:11	125
2:17	125
3:5	125
3:12	126
3:21	126
4:11	22
15:3,4	77
21:1,23	86
21:3,4	12
21:7	126

Index of First Lines of Hymns

A mighty fortress is our God	43
At even, when the sun was set	50
Christ, whose glory fills the skies	87
Come, thou almighty King	69
Father eternal, Ruler of creation	42
God is my strong salvation	104
God is working his purpose out	14
Great God who hast delivered us	28
Guide, me, O thou great Jehovah	46
Have thine own way, Lord	96
High o'er the lonely hills	82
How firm a foundation, ye saints of the Lord	25
I heard an old, old story	128
If thou but suffer God to guide thee	45
Immortal, invisible, God only wise	71
In heavenly love abiding	113
In the hour of trial	116
Jesus, Lover of my soul	105
Joyful, joyful, we adore thee	19
Lead on, O King eternal	74
Lead us, O Father, in the paths of peace	33
Lord of all being, throned afar	78
Lord divine, all loves excelling	22
My faith looks up to thee	118
My God, I thank thee, who hast made	65
Now thank we all our God	12
O God, our help in ages past	15
O Master, let me walk with thee	91
O worship the King, all glorious above	75
Praise, my soul, the King of heaven	77
Savior, thy dying love	110
Saviour, like a shepherd lead us	111
Saviour, teach me, day by day	114
Spirit of God, descend upon my heart	121
This is my Father's world	39
What a friend we have in Jesus	17
Who trusts in God, a strong abode	32

Acknowledgments

The editor and the publisher have made every effort to trace the ownership of all copyrighted material and to secure permission from copyright holders of such material. In the event of any question arising as to the use of any material the publisher and editor, while expressing regret for inadvertent error, will be pleased to make the necessary corrections in future printings. Thanks are due to the following authors, publishers, publications and agents for permission to use the material indicated.

ABINGDON PRESS, for excerpts by Dr. Lynn Hough from *The Interpreter's Bible,* Volume 12, copyright © 1957 by Abingdon Press.

HARPER & ROW, PUBLISHERS, INC., for excerpts from *The New Harper's Bible Dictionary,* 8th Revised edition by Madeleine S. and J. Lane Miller, copyright © 1973 by Harper & Row, Publishers, Inc.

MOODY PRESS, for "Waiting on God" by Andrew Murray.

OXFORD UNIVERSITY PRESS, for "High O'er the Lonely Hills" by Jan Struther, from *Enlarged Songs of Praise.*

CHARLES SCRIBNER'S SONS, for "Joyful, Joyful, We Adore Thee" from *The Complete Poems of Henry Van Dyke.*

THE SEABURY PRESS, for "From Everlasting to Everlasting" by Florence M. Taylor, copyright © 1973 by Florence M. Taylor.

THE VIKING PRESS, INC., for "Prayer at Sunrise" from *Saint Peter Relates an Incident* by James Weldon Johnson, copyright 1917, renewed © 1963 by Grace Nail Johnson.